Schibsted

This is the first book of its kind to examine Schibsted, one of the largest traditional media and newspaper companies in the Nordic region, which is today considered a regional and international digital media pioneer.

The book examines the rise and role of Schibsted – an early mover and proactive media company in terms of technology adoption, digitization, and online expansion – in its home region, along with its major international ventures. The book focuses on its position in the Nordic digital media landscape, one of the world's most digitally mature media markets and most digitally networked region, which is today influenced by fierce competition from expanding global Internet giants and platform infrastructure. Drawing on a wealth of sources, including original interviews with senior Schibsted executives, which allow unprecedented insight into the company, the book also details its digital expansion internationally, and particularly its pioneering role as originator of the world's largest online classified advertising company.

This book will be of interest to students and scholars of global media and communication studies, particularly those specializing in international communication and media industries in a global context.

Ole J. Mjøs is a Professor in Media Studies in the Department of Information Science and Media Studies, University of Bergen, Norway. He specializes in the fields of international communication and global media. He is the author of *An Introduction to Global Media for the Twenty-First Century* (2023), *Music, Social Media and Global Mobility* (2012), and *Media Globalization and the Discovery Channel Networks* (2010) and is co-author of *The Media Welfare State: Nordic Media in the Digital Era* (2014). He has been a visiting scholar at the Center for Global Communication Studies, Annenberg School for Communication, University of Pennsylvania, USA, and a visiting researcher at the Centre for Mobilities Research, Lancaster University, UK.

Global Media Giants
Series editors: Benjamin J. Birkinbine,
Rodrigo Gomez and Janet Wasko

Since the second half of the 20th century, the significance of media corporate power has been increasing in different and complex ways around the world; the power of these companies in political, symbolic and economic terms has been a global issue and concern. In the 21st century, understanding media corporations is essential to understanding the political, economic and socio-cultural dimensions of our contemporary societies.

The **Global Media Giants** series continues the work that began in the series editors' book *Global Media Giants*, providing detailed examinations of the largest and most powerful media corporations in the world.

Bertelsmann
A Transnational Media Service Giant
Mandy Tröger and Jörg Becker

Baidu
Geopolitical Dynamics of the Internet in China
ShinJoung Yeo

Nintendo
Playing with Power
Randy Nichols

News Corp
Empire of Influence
Graham Murdock, Benedetta Brevini and Michael Ward

Schibsted
The Digital Transformation of a Nordic Media Giant
Ole J. Mjøs

For more information about this series, please visit: https://www.routledge.com/Global-Media-Giants/book-series/GMG

Schibsted
The Digital Transformation of a Nordic Media Giant

Ole J. Mjøs

NEW YORK AND LONDON

First published 2025
by Routledge
605 Third Avenue, New York, NY 10158

and by Routledge
4 Park Square, Milton Park, Abingdon, Oxon, OX14 4RN

Routledge is an imprint of the Taylor & Francis Group, an informa business

© 2025 Ole J. Mjos

The right of Ole J. Mjos to be identified as author of this work has been asserted in accordance with sections 77 and 78 of the Copyright, Designs and Patents Act 1988.

All rights reserved. No part of this book may be reprinted or reproduced or utilised in any form or by any electronic, mechanical, or other means, now known or hereafter invented, including photocopying and recording, or in any information storage or retrieval system, without permission in writing from the publishers.

Trademark notice: Product or corporate names may be trademarks or registered trademarks, and are used only for identification and explanation without intent to infringe.

ISBN: 978-1-032-57451-6 (hbk)
ISBN: 978-1-032-57453-0 (pbk)
ISBN: 978-1-003-43943-1 (ebk)

DOI: 10.4324/9781003439431

Typeset in Times New Roman
by Apex CoVantage, LLC

To Mari and Frida

Contents

	List of Interviewees	*viii*
1	Introduction	1
2	The Formation of the Modern Schibsted and Pioneering the Digital and International Expansion: 1989–2000	14
3	The Emergence of the Digital and International Schibsted: 2000–2009	38
4	Streamlining, New Digital Business Models, and Global Ambitions: 2009–2014	61
5	In the Face of Global Platformization: The Ecosystem Strategy: 2014–2017	82
6	The World's Largest Online Classified Company, the Schibsted Universe, and the Splitting of the Company: 2017–2025	97
7	Concluding Remarks – The Regional Perspective	120
	References	*126*
	Index	*134*

Interviewees

Interviewees and their key positions within Schibsted and the Tinius Trust and other relevant positions. Between 1 and 3 interviews were conducted with each interviewee. All interviewees have spoken their native language, Norwegian or Swedish, during the interviews, and the author has made the translations of the majority of them into English.

Trine Eilertsen, Editor-in-Chief and Chief Executive Officer (CEO) of *Aftenposten* since 2020, and Political Editor 2014–2020; Editor-in-Chief of *Bergens Tidende*, 2008–2012, and Political Editor, 2002–2008.

Sondre Gravir, Board member Schibsted Media, 2024–; employed at Schibsted, 2007–2018; former CEO of Schibsted Marketplaces; Executive Vice President (EVP) of Schibsted Established Markets; and CEO of FINN, *Aftenposten* and *Bergens Tidende*; former McKinsey consultant.

Raoul Grünthal, employed at Schibsted from 2006 until 2021; EVP of Schibsted Next, 2018–2021; Head of Schibsted Media, 2017–2018; CEO and EVP of Schibsted Sverige, 2009–2017; CEO of Schibsted's News Media division; CEO of *Svenska Dagbladet* and *Aftonbladet*.

Christian Printzell Halvorsen, CEO of Schibsted Marketplaces from 2024, senior positions within Schibsted's marketplaces operations for more than ten years, including as CEO of FINN and Senior Vice President (SVP) Product in Schibsted Marketplaces before the Adevinta spin-off in 2019; former McKinsey consultant.

Anne Langbraaten, Economist at *Verdens Gang* (*VG*) before joining Schibsted in 1989 as Finance Manager; director of finance of Schibsted Nett in 1996 and later Chief Financial Officer (CFO) of *Scandinavia Online* until 2001.

Kristin Løken Stavrum, CEO at the Tinius Trust, 2016–; Chair of the Board of Schibsted Media, 2024–, and Member of the Board of the Tinius Trust; former Chair of the Board of Blommenholm Industrier; former feature editor, and editor of the A magazine and the Aften edition of Aftenposten, 2005–2012.

Kristin Skogen Lund, CEO of Schibsted, 2018–2024; CEO of Telenor, 2010–2012, publisher and CEO of *Aftenposten*, 2007–2010; CEO and Chief Editor of *Scandinavia Online*, 1998–2002.

Interviewees ix

Torry Pedersen, former Managing Editor in *VG*; Editor-in-Chief/publisher in *VG Multimedia* AS; CEO of *VG AS* and from 2011 both CEO and Editor-in-Chief of *VG AS* until 2017; head of publishing at Schibsted Norway, 2017–2019.

Birger Magnus, Deputy CEO of Schibsted and EVP of News of Schibsted, 1996–2009; former Chairman and Director of *VG* and *Aftenposten*, Media Norge, and Schibsted Norge; chairman of *Aftonbladet* Hierta AB, Handelsbolaget *Svenska Dagbladet*s AB & Co, and 20 Min Holding AG; from 1985 to 1995, partner and principal for Norway in McKinsey & Co.; managing partner, Oslo office, in the latter part, as well as leading partner in McKinsey's international multimedia practice.

Didrik Munch, former CEO and EVP of Schibsted Norge, 2012–2018; CEO of Media Norge 2008–2012; CEO of *Bergens Tidende* 1997–2008; former Chairman of FINN, Schibsted Growth, and Schibsted's newspapers in Norway.

Sverre Munck, EVP of Schibsted Media Group, 1996–2013; CFO of Schibsted in 1994, and EVP Multimedia in 1996; in 2006, responsible for international operations as EVP Strategy and International; former McKinsey consultant.

Aleksander Rosinski, Advisor to Schibsted Marketplaces and non-executive director of Adevinta from 2019; Vice President of Telenor Digital overseeing online classified advertising investments in Asia and South America, 2012–2019; former board member of Blocket, *VG Multimedia*, OLX in Brazil and Adevinta; Managing Director of FINN Travel.

Rolv Erik Ryssdal, Board member, Schibsted Marketplace, 2024–; CEO of Adevinta ASA 2018–2023; CEO of Schibsted Media Group, 2009–2018; CEO of Schibsted Classified Media, 2008–2009; CEO of *VG*, 2005–2008; CEO of *Aftonbladet*, 1999–2005; Director, finance and HR of *Aftonbladet* 1997–1999; CFO of Schibsted 1994–1997; corporate secretary at Schibsted, 1993–1996; consultant and project manager of initial public offerings (IPOs) at Schibsted, 1991–1993.

Terje Seljeseth, Chief Analyst, Tinius Trust and Blommenholm Industrier, 2017–2020. Various positions within Schibsted for 33 years, former EVP Chief Product Officer and EVP Product Management of Schibsted, 2015–2017; CEO of Schibsted Classified Media (SCM), 2009–2015, as well as starting FINN in 1999 and managing the company for 10 years.

Gard Steiro, Editor-in-Chief and CEO of *VG*, 2017–present. Editor-in-Chief of *Bergens Tidende*, 2015–2017; Board member Polaris Media (2024–).

Ole Jacob Sunde, Chair of the Board of Schibsted from 2002 to 2022 and Board member of Schibsted in 2000–2002. Board member since the inception in 1996 of the Tinius Trust and Chair of the Board since 2007. Chair of the Scott Trust, owner of *The Guardian* and *The Observer* since 2021. McKinsey consultant, 1980–1983.

Siv Juvik Tveitnes, CEO of Schibsted Media from 2024, EVP News Media from 2019. Previously Chief Operating Officer of Schibsted Media,

x *Interviewees*

chairman of the board of directors of *Aftonbladet* and *Svenska Dagbladet*; CEO of *Bergens Tidende* and *Stavanger Aftenblad*; Project Director at Media Norge.

Kjell Aamot, CEO of Schibsted, 1989–2010, CFO and CEO of *VG*, 1977–1989. Chairman of Aftenposten, *VG*, Schibsted Film, a.o.

1 Introduction

This is the first book on the digital transformation and international expansion of Schibsted, one of the largest news and media companies in the Nordic region and originator of the world's largest online classified operations. Founded in 1839 as a book-printing company by Christian Schibsted in Oslo, Norway, Schibsted turned into a key Norwegian newspaper company throughout the twentieth century and expanded into a Scandinavian media conglomerate with major TV and film holdings from the early 1990s. In the mid-1990s, the company became a digital pioneer, focusing on expanding its legacy news media brands and advertising business online also to protect its position against international competition in the expanding digital domain. It launched the first Internet portal for the Scandinavian region, *Scandinavia Online*, which became the most popular website in Norway and Sweden in 1998. In 2000, Schibsted established its own Norwegian online classified advertising company. In doing so, Schibsted is arguably the only major news company that succeeded in transferring its traditional print classified advertising business online (Anand and Hood, 2007; Norland, 2011; Syvertsen et al., 2014). Still, it was controversial, as it cannibalized the classified income of its own print newspapers. This spurred the development of what would later become the world's largest online classified advertising company, Adevinta. Then, faced with early competition from Google and Facebook, Schibsted stood out among the Nordic media companies through its comprehensive strategies to compete with these platforms. Schibsted launched its own regional search engine, *Sesam*, and a social media service, *Nettby*, in the 2000s, and it aimed to create a global online classified platform and digital media and advertising platforms across its Norwegian and Swedish news brands in the 2010s. In 2023, Schibsted had a predominantly Nordic presence with over 6,000 employees, around NOK 16 billion in revenues, over 60 brands, 3.6 million daily logged-in users, its news media reaching 80 percent of the Norwegian and Swedish population weekly, and it had a 28.1 percent ownership in Adevinta (Schibsted, 2023a).

In late 2023, Schibsted announced changes that led to arguably the most dramatic events in its history: the company split up. The peculiar combination of being stock-listed and trust-owned is key to understanding Schibsted's digital transformation and international expansion. The Norwegian Tinius Trust has

DOI: 10.4324/9781003439431-1

2   *Schibsted*

been the largest shareholder, with Articles of Association emphasizing a focus on news media, and has had negative control of the company that was stock-listed in 1992. The Trust contributed to the company's long-term thinking and protection against foreign takeover (Syvertsen et al., 2014), while also exposing the company to the more restless, impatient and unpredictable global market. This created a key dynamic for its digital transformation and international expansion. Schibsted has developed through a series of acquisitions, mergers, divestments, and reorganizations, and the splitting of the company is the latest, most significant twist. In 2024, the Tinius Trust, acquired Schibsted's Norwegian and Swedish media assets for NOK 6.2 billion, taking them off the market, while the Nordic online marketplace operations continued as a publicly traded company as Schibsted Marketplace. Schibsted sold major shareholdings in the global online classified advertising company it originated, Adevinta, which was valued at NOK 141 billion, but it remained a key owner, and shareholders received NOK 20 billion in cash dividend from the transaction. This enabled Schibsted's main owner, the Tinius Trust, through its holding company Blommenholm Industrier, to acquire all the company's media assets, soon followed by major television acquisitions in Sweden and Finland, in 2025. In this way, the Tinius Trust became the sole owner of one of the largest media groups in the region. At the same time, the Tinius Trust owns around 22 per cent of the total shares, but nearly 30 percent of the voting rights, in the remaining stock listed Schibsted Marketplaces, which in turn owns around 14 percent of the global online classified advertising company, Adevinta.

This book tells the story of Schibsted through original research and access to unique empirical materials. The book draws on the author's personal interviews with former and current Schibsted and Tinius Trust employees at senior executive, and board levels, including all the CEOs of Schibsted from 1989 to 2025, throughout the company's digital transformation and international expansion, while combining this material with corporate and public information and relevant research. Most of the interviewees have worked for Schibsted for many years, and their accounts and reflections offer an entry point to capture their perspective on Schibsted's development during this 35-year period. While this comprehensive story is fascinating – and so far, untold in book-length form – this book also provides theoretical contributions. It critically applies perspectives from within media and communications to explain the story of Schibsted from the field of international communication and global media, as well as media economics and management studies.

The book argues that we can understand the case of the digital transformation and international expansion of Schibsted by looking at a set of dimensions related to the company, its leadership and the external context. The case of Schibsted is also important as it sheds further light on the global–local dichotomy. Schibsted is situated at the heart of the study of the internationalization and globalization of media and communication, and it exemplifies how regionalization plays out in the global media landscape. Schibsted's successful digital transformation is also due to the external conditions, the Nordic media market and system, which is the world's most digitally mature media market and with among the most digitally networked

Introduction 3

nations: Norway, Sweden, Denmark, Finland and Iceland. Collectively, the region has a population of just under 30 million and features some of the world's highest adoption rates of digital media and technology. Traditionally, the region has the world's highest level of press freedom and freedom of speech, and the population of the region has been the most avid news consumers. The level of trust in news in the region stands out, and news sites are primary news sources, compared to other parts of world where social media and search and aggregators are increasingly preferred news destinations (Syvertsen et al., 2014; Newman et al., 2024; DESI, 2022; Lindberg, 2023; RSF, 2024). The book argues that Schibsted has benefited from, been shaped by, and contributed to shaping the region's distinct media system, described as the *Media Welfare State* (Syvertsen et al., 2014) and thereby also played a role in the societal, political, and cultural development of the region. Schibsted has defined itself as a protector and champion of free speech and press freedom in the region, and some have labeled the company a "cornerstone institution" (2014: 100). This book, then, critically examines the development, role, and position of Schibsted throughout its digital transformation and international expansion until 2025. However, the story of Schibsted also involves concerns over the company's media and economic power, a critique of its dominance in news, fears of loss of media diversity, internal disputes and unrest, and the high risks and costly failures of digital innovations and investments.

THE FOUR PHASES IN NORDIC MEDIA MARKET

The general developments and trends of the global media landscape shape and influence the Nordic media market and the news sector. Yet, the region's media also has its distinctiveness and characteristics that defines it and in many ways sets it apart. This book builds on descriptions of key developments of Schibsted's digital transformation and internationalization, as described by Syvertsen et al. (2014), who situate this development within three phases in the region's media market, and this book proposes a fourth key phase.

In the *first phase*, throughout the 1970s and 1980s, media companies began to diversify, making investments and acquisitions outside their principal areas of business. At the same time, companies outside of media began to expand into media (Syvertsen et al., 2014: 98; Hjeltnes, 2010). In the *second phase*, 1990s and early 2000, these developments evolved and intensified as deregulation, liberalization, and privatization of telecommunication and television, and later online markets, led to the "opening up" of markets and sectors (Sundin, 2013: 9). Media companies expanded horizontally, vertically, and diagonally into new business areas, for example, newspaper companies moved into television nationally and internationally, as also the growing ambitions outside the Nordic region was increasingly evident (Doyle, 2013, 2016; Syvertsen et al., 2014; Eide, 1995).

The *third phase* is characterized by the increased focus on core business areas and the expansion of these areas, while divesting from and moving out of non-core businesses (Syvertsen et al., 2014). In the Nordic region, this phase began around 2005: "Most of the large Nordic media groups have since then

4 *Schibsted*

clearly changed their strategy. They no longer expand their operations, but increasingly concentrate on a few core areas and wind down more peripheral operations" (Sundin, 2013: 10). Spurred by the financial crises in 2008/2009, divestment of non-core assets and less diagonal expansion went hand in hand with the more focused vertical and horizontal investments and expansion within core business areas, and the international expansion in the core areas continued.

The *fourth phase*, from the early 2010s in the aftermath of the financial crisis, companies continued consolidation, cost-cutting, and focus on core business areas nationally and internationally were paired with the search for digital business models. Online newspapers sought to find subscription models since the 1990s and traditional business models, particularly in print media, were increasingly under threat (Krumsvik, 2014; Lowe, 2016: 8). These challenges intensified in the Nordic region by the increased competition of the global platform giants, part of the wider process of platformization (Poell et al., 2019, 2021).

In the mid-2010s, digital advertisements were considered by many companies as a solution. By increasing online traffic, one would attract advertisers, and this would finance journalism. While advertisers did shift their spending to the online environment, their investments went increasingly to global platforms. Therefore, in the latter half of the 2010s and the early 2020s, most paid newspapers implemented different forms of digital user payment for subscriptions and other services (Lindberg, 2023: 88). In fact, the year 2013 has been dubbed by some "the year of the paywall," as digital subscription solutions were introduced widely (Sjovaag, 2015: 304). However, since the mid-2010s, the "data-driven platform economy" transformed the news sector (Sjovaag, 2023: 3). Facing intense competition from Google and Facebook, Nordic media have countered by either making their own platforms or collaborating with the global platforms, to develop their business models (Sundet and Ihlebæk; Mjos, 2022; Eide and Myrvang, 2018). Since the mid-2010s, the platform firms have both strengthened and grown not only their advertising market shares but also their position as an infrastructure for news distribution (Lindberg, 2023: 88). They also launched several news-related products to compete directly with publishers (Nielsen and Ganter, 2022). Still, the position and impact of these global platforms on the news media sector differ across the world. In the Nordic region, readers continue to access news media outlets directly, in contrast to international developents as global platforms have increasingly become primary news destinations (Sjovaag, 2023; Newman et al., 2024).

The Global–Local Dichotomy: International Communications and Global Media Studies

The study of international communication and global media has historically "shifted uneasily between a focus on the global scale of communication and upon the nation-state as its primary site of analysis and engagement" (Flew et al., 2016: 4). The analysis of Schibsted is situated between these two viewpoints, as the book shows how Schibsted is a significant example of how regionalization plays

Introduction 5

out between the local/national and the global. The study of Schibsted allows us to understand the company from within its country-of-origin, Norway, across the Nordic region, and then outside the region as well as its international expansion. These perspectives will be discussed in the final chapter, as we situate the company's corporate strategies and their operationalization throughout its digital transformation and international expansion, within the regional perspective.

A Critical Perspective on Corporate Strategy and Its Dimensions

The book tells the story of Schibsted's digital and international expansion and shows how three categories of dimensions – external, leadership, and company dimensions – mutually shape and influence the processes of strategy-making and implementation. The book thereby aims to understand "media transformation" in relation to digitization and internationalization by approaching the often unclear "concept of transformation" by dividing or breaking down "the selected contributions to concrete areas of change made visible through inter- and transdisciplinary research approaches from different perspectives" (Godulla and Böhm, 2023: 2). This is of particular importance, in relation to the media industries, as they differ from other industries since they are not only profit-seeking industries but also have several "social responsibilities and a degree of social impact that seems exceptional" (Lowe, 2016: 5). In fact, its societal role and influence are often viewed as "wildly disproportionate to their economic worth" (Gourevitch and Deslandes, 2024: 4). As the pace of digitization intensified, the news sector role has been challenged by rapid changes as its income decreased dramatically and its traditional business model has been increasingly considered as unsustainable (Picard, 2010: 365). This trend has intensified into the 2020s as user patterns shift, editorial and financial models are overturned, and competition from global players has increased dramatically (Gourevitch and Deslandes, 2024: 4).

Media companies, their managers, and stakeholders face a complex digital environment characterized by considerable economies of scale, convergence of industries and technologies, a high failure rate of products and services, a market characterized by network effects, and a "winner-takes-all" environment (Noam, 2019: 631) and the "hit-or-miss nature" of the media business (Doyle, 2016: 185). While the industry is facing major challenges, so too do researchers who grapple with how to explain these developments. Furthermore, the media industry is an umbrella term for a "group of disparate industries that have content creation and dissemination as their central activity," and its definition is further complicated as the technology sector has increasingly become part of the media industry (Küng, 2016: 277). Therefore, as the definition of the media industry is complex, so too is corporate strategy-making (Oliver and Picard, 2020: 67).

The challenges for both media managers and researchers are of significance for this book, as it draws to a large extent on the perspective of senior

6 *Schibsted*

executives and their strategy-making decisions, and implementation of these strategies. A fruitful starting point, then, is to look closely at how corporate strategy planning in large media companies is done and who and what influences this process. Corporate strategies are often planned by the Chief Executive Officer (CEO), the top-level management, and/or the board. News media companies must also consider and respect editorial independence, freedom, and power. Strategies may also be influenced by outside experts such as management consultancies. In addition, shareholders may try to exert influence on a company's direction. Strategies can be shaped by a specialized and dedicated corporate strategy group centrally or a more radical approach where strategic planning and decisions are decentralized (Noam, 2019: 642). While the advantages of a centralized approach may give company-wide control, coordination, and long-term planning, the disadvantages are the "distance from the actual experiences of divisions and functional tasks". The opposite of the top-down approach is the decentralized approach, which may be described as more bottom-up. In its most drastic version, this may involve the different divisions deciding their own "autonomous strategy." In this case, those in charge of strategic decision-making benefit from their proximity and insight into the specific markets where they wish to succeed. However, large media companies often use a mixed strategy approach.

The External, Leadership, and Company Dimensions of Corporate Strategy for the Digital Transformation and International Expansion

The dynamic between centralization and decentralization in corporate strategy-making and its implementation is shaped and influenced by different dimensions. These dimensions can be grouped into three categories: (1) external dimensions, including the media system and media market; (2) leadership dimensions, including the style of management, corporate culture, influence of global consultancies; and (3) company dimensions, including the ownership structure and form, organizational structure, capital, and financial conditions (see Figure 1.1).

The External Dimensions

The Media System

Traditionally, the Nordic region is defined as a Northern Europe democratic corporatist media system (Hallin and Mancini, 2004). Yet Syvertsen et al. (2014) call for a more detailed and nuanced, regional-specific definition. The authors argue the Nordic region's media system mirrors the characteristics of the strong welfare states of the region's countries, and this sets it apart internationally. This media system, the *Media Welfare State*, aims to counter the forces

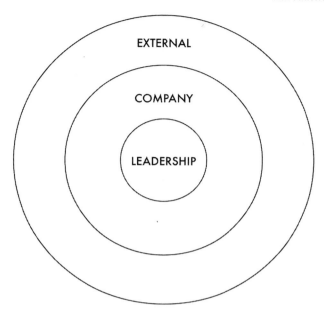

Figure 1.1 The Dimensions: External, Company and Leadership

of globalization, authoritarianism, and marketization through four policy measures: the organization of key communication services in line with the concept of public goods with subsidies and requirements fostering universal access; institutionalizing press freedom, media policies that support media to ensure media diversity and quality, and; collaboration and consensus between key public and private stakeholders, that is, media companies and the state. Historically, media companies in the region benefit from these measures in the form of press subsidies and tax exemption for newspapers, the traditionally high levels of press freedom, freedom of speech, and news consumption, and importantly, the region's digital infrastructure. The regions' policymakers considered from early on the development of universal access to advanced Internet services as the key to economic and social progress (Syvertsen et al., 2014; Enli et al., 2018).

Media Market and Competition

Market competition is one of the key dimensions influencing the dynamic between centralization and decentralization within media and newspaper companies. In the newspaper market, the traditional business model of selling physical copies of newspapers and cross-financing journalism through monetizing

8 *Schibsted*

the readers through print advertising clashed with the characteristics of digitization and Internet (O'Brian, 2024: 431). Newspapers saw their traditional way of generating revenue from this two-sided business model increasingly under pressure. As the financial crisis in 2008 hit, news companies decided to streamline and consolidate their businesses focusing on core areas (Sjovaag, 2019). A key strategic response to the combination of technological and economic conditions was chain ownership of newspapers (Sjovaag, 2014). Since the mid-2010s, size increasingly mattered, as the maturing digital market rewarded large structures with economies of scale and network effects (Lindberg, 2023). Media companies need to respond to the fact that "[c]ompetition in the media and communications industry is becoming global, as local, regional, national, and the major globally expanding media and communications companies all move online" (Mjos, 2022: 4). The global platforms have inserted themselves between news producers and consumers and thereby influence how news is distributed, consumed, and monetized (Westlund et al., 2020: 5). These intermediary platforms "shape the media ecology, editorial organizations have tried their best to reap the benefits of these changes looking for opportunities to survive as their markets change" (Sjovaag, 2023: 5).

The Leadership Dimensions

The Style of Management

Media market trends are often seen as the key influence on the actions of media executives, but media leaders also exercise agency. They have different motivations, may be proactive or more passive, and their relations with the owners may differ. Some may favor central control and a strong corporate brand, while others may be more inclined to let individual businesses and brands operate independently. These dynamics can influence the way corporate strategy is created and implemented. Furthermore, the processes of digitization demand more from managers than "managing in a traditional sense," as succeeding in business relies on the company's capacity to adjust quickly to the developments and shifting characteristics of the digital economy. This has led to an increased focus on media executives' ability to be entrepreneurial (Artero and Manfredi, 2016: 57). Management in the digital economy therefore demands a balance of traditional media business models and innovative approaches to support new initiatives.

Traditional theories of the firm argue that "a commercial firm's every decision is taken in order to maximize profits," but in terms of media companies this can be criticized by two views. The first is that "it is too crude and simplistic to assume that businesses are motivated purely by pursuit of profits," as the motives for owning media companies may be, for example, "the pursuit of public and political influence" (Doyle, 2013: 5). The second criticism of the theory of the purely profit-motivated firm "assumes that all firms will behave in the same way, irrespective of their size and organizational structure" (Doyle, 2013: 5). However, as ownership, influence, and control over a company may be divided, managers may also work toward goals that are not necessarily in line with shareholders preferences. One example may be that "the pursuit of profits may be superseded by for example a desire to maximize sales revenue or the company's growth" (Doyle, 2013: 6). The "Principal-Agent Problem" is at the heart of these tensions and may emerge as "decision-making authority is delegated to managers as Agents employed by the Principals (owners) to run increasingly large and diversified international media firms" (Artero and Manfredi, 2016: 53).

Corporate Culture

Corporate cultures are also an important element in understanding "power relations in media organisations" (Deslades, 2016: 320). Media companies may have a hierarchical structure, but they often set themselves apart from other industries, as the power relations between managers, employees, and owners may be unclear or leadership issues may be difficult to comprehend (Deslades, 2016: 313). Corporate or organizational culture may be an "intangible concept," yet it affects the people and the operations of a company in establishing norms and values that guide how work is done within the company over time (Golnaz Sadri and Lees, 2001: 853).

Corporate culture is influenced by several factors, including "the industry in which the company operates, its geographic location, events that have occurred during its history, the personalities of its employees, and their patterns of interaction" (Golnaz Sadri and Lees, 2001: 854). Many large news companies facing digitization have become technology companies as well. These companies may therefore combine journalistic and editorial content as well as business, and technology development. As such, they integrate a diverse set of corporate cultures, including the interplay and tension between them.

Global Management Consultancies

The dynamic between centralization and decentralization in corporate strategy and its implementation is also often shaped by advice to senior management from influential global management consultancies. Centralization may relate to how such consultancies promote and recommend global industry trends that are implemented in individual companies. Traditionally, these consultancies operate as external professionals that focus on strategic planning to assist organizations in making changes to improve or achieve value creation (Kraaijenbrink, 2020: 8). The most well-known consultancies include Boston Consulting Group, Bain & Company, and McKinsey & Company, each with specialized divisions or practices according to industry, including media, communications

10 *Schibsted*

and technology. Yet these consultancies have been criticized for several reasons, including legitimizing decision-making, lack of integrative view, project-based instead of process-based, lack of diversity, no liability and risk, profit-oriented, self-centered, creating dependence, and selling fads (Kraaijenbrink, 2020: 24–28). Historically, one key critique has been that these consultancies advise and implement changes within companies, yet, at the same time are in "constant search for new models to be commodified and resold to the large organizations that are already clients of the consultants" (McKenna, 2012: 155).

The Company Dimensions

The Ownership Structure and form

The ownership structure and form of large media companies also shape the dynamic between centralization and decentralization in the corporate strategy-making and implementation. The form of ownership also influences the running of large news companies and their editorial production and output (Benson et. al., 2025). In recent years, foundations and trusts have been the most proactive in acquiring newspapers in the Nordic region (Sjovaag, 2023). While the largest Nordic newspaper company by revenue in 2021, Bonnier News (SE), part of the family-owned Bonnier group, five of the ten largest newspaper companies across the Nordic region, JP/Politikens HUS (DK), Amedia (NO), Jysk Fynske Medier (DK), Norrköpings Tidningars Media (SE), and Gota Media (SE) were all either fully owned or majority-owned by foundations or trusts, and the second and the third largest, Schibsted News Media, at the time, and Sanoma Media Finland respectively, were part of larger publicly traded company groups, that had trusts as the largest single shareholder (Lindberg, 2023: 34–35). Investors and the stock market may lead to unpredictable ownership structures as well as pressures and expectations from investors, but "trust and foundation ownership is thought to entail more relaxed profit expectations, long-term operational security, and to an extent a more 'ideal' form of ownership" (Sjovaag and Ohlsson, 2019: 9). Still, even companies owned by a nonprofit foundation are not exempted from running the company in line with for-profit principles (Sjovaag and Ohlsson, 2019: 13). However, such companies may have lower demands for financial return than a stock-listed company.

There are several advantages of foundation ownership. A study of three business foundations in the Swedish newspaper sector found such ownership "provides companies with stability and a long-term strategic intent, where strategic decisions are not restricted by the demand for quick payoffs" (Achtenhagen et al., 2018: 146). Furthermore, the stability provided by foundation ownership prevents the newspapers from being taken over by others. Still, foundation ownership also comes with a possible weakness, if the board and top management lack relevant business competence. However, foundations with high competence

Introduction 11

are "outperforming their peers" (Achtenhagen et al., 2018: 147) even if foundation ownership set limits for financial growth and expansion "since the foundations' original holdings cannot be sold, and their original capital cannot be easily diluted" (Achtenhagen et al., 2018: 147). However, if a company has a mixed ownership, it may create tension in the dynamic between centralization and decentralization. The trust or foundation's charter or Articles of Association are at the heart of the corporate strategies of the company, while at the same time the company is exposed to the global capital market and investors.

Organizational Structure

This dimension relates to the organization of large, expanding media companies, and the central corporate headquarters in relation to its various brands, susidiaries and companies. This dimension is relevant both to businesses in the home market and when expanding internationally. Hermanni (2023) identifies a set of motives or "triggers" for international expansion of media companies in the digital era: potential for growth in the home market is limited, while the growth potential internationally is significant; digital media products can be reproduced cost-efficiently and adapted for export; the increase in the market value of companies; and risk reduction through spreading of risk internationally (2023: 6).

International expansion can take place through vertical, horizontal, and diagonal expansion. Horizontal expansion happens when two companies with the same activity in the same sector and in the same position in the supply chain are combined or merged. This approach may increase the market share and give economic benefits. Such expansion has therefore the potential to create economies of scale and is therefore appealing within the media sector. Vertical expansion happens when a company makes acquisitions throughout the stages of the supply chain. Diagonal expansion, also called "conglomerate expansion," happens when a company expands into a new business area. The advantages of diagonal expansion may be economic, the creation of synergies, and risk diversification (Doyle, 2013: 36–37, 2016: 182–183).

These diverse ways of expanding relate to the dynamic between centralization and decentralization in the corporate strategy-making and implementation. On the one hand, it may be the case that as media companies expand internationally, their management structure becomes increasingly decentralized (Doyle, 2013: 37). Media companies may expand internationally through launching new businesses and letting them develop independently or by acquiring already-established companies and letting them continue to develop within their specific media market context while being part of a corporate structure (Mjøs, 2010, 2022). On the other hand, the rise of global platforms through a combination of global expansion, centralized strategies, ecosystem, global products, and economies of scale, has taken expansion to an unprecedented level. In terms of technology, global media platforms expand

12　*Schibsted*

with the same technology, while media companies that expand through either organic growth or mergers and acquisitions may have to work around different technologies as they expand. This is certainly an advantage with a centralized approach in terms of achieving economies of scale, as the "asymmetrical power relations" between the global platform companies and media companies particularly in smaller countries become increasingly evident (Ihlebæk and Sundet, 2021: 2184).

Capital and Financial Conditions

The financial condition of a company, and the financial resources it generates and controls, has a major impact on the company's corporate strategy, as revenue provides the income to run the business. Since around 2000, publicly traded companies focusing on news were considered "a highly risky choice for investors" in comparison to other sectors (Picard, 2010: 376). Around 2010s, newspapers scrambled to find viable revenue and online business models, as online advertising was not generating enough income to sustain news production. As such, capital and revenues were considered the main challenges for managers of news companies and organizations. While the belief in online advertising was also waning in the Nordic region, in the second half of the 2010s and early 2020s, most paid newspapers developed different forms of digital payment solutions, either for subscriptions or for other kinds of services (Lindberg, 2023: 88). By 2023, the major newspapers that were part of the big groups in the large Nordic countries have been among those with most success in terms of attracting both users and advertisers to pay for digital journalism (Lindberg, 2023: 89).

A key issue is the resource allocation within a large media company (Doyle, 2016), for example, the transfer of profits from individual companies to the mother company. The question is when to allocate investments and profits to the best of the company as a whole or for individual or groups of companies? A further question is what should the core areas of business be, and what is the priority between them? In times of high levels of revenue and profit, expansion may be possible and be easier to justify, while in times of financial constraints the company may need to cut costs, contract, consolidate, and downsize. The latter may certainly create tension between the central and the decentralized parts of the company.

Innovation

Innovation is the key to any corporate strategy and its successful implementation, as "[t]he corporate mission also enables a sense of dynamism within the company, since innovation is required if long-term goals are to be met"

(Medina et al., 2016: 249). In fact, Noam (2019) argues that "perhaps the main factor for strategy is rapid technological change in this sector." As a digitizing media and communications industry has increasingly faced forms of "radical disruption" (Noam, 2019: 631). From the perspective of "creative destruction," Doyle argues that there are severe consequences for large incumbent media companies that do not adapt to technological change and exploit new opportunities through innovation, as they are weakened and then destroyed at the end (2013: 26). However, macro processes such as financial crises and recessions also play a role in the process of "creative destruction" in terms of allocating resources from less profitable business activities and intensify the "pace at which slow adaptors get weeded out" (Doyle, 2013: 28).

A broader understanding of innovation, not limited to technology, is of significance here. The concept of "media innovation" suggests a wider approach to innovation that may include "the development of new media platforms to new business models, to new ways of producing media texts" (Storsul and Krumsvik, 2013: 16). As such, a media innovation perspective focuses on novel and new media forms, developments in media production, and distribution and consumption patterns and practices (Ibrus, 2024: 44). A more overarching form of innovation is organizational innovation, including the ability to adapt and develop an organization that can initiate, support, and drive various innovation processes taking place within the organization or company itself.

2 The Formation of the Modern Schibsted and Pioneering the Digital and International Expansion

1989–2000

This chapter traces the historical origins of Schibsted and then details its corporatization in the late 1980s as a major Norwegian newspaper company, and the following stock listing in 1992. In the wake of the listing, ambitions within the company and expectations from investors led to horizontal, vertical, and diagonal expansions into film and television and, from the mid-1990s, into multimedia and international markets. The emerging online domain opened for new competition from international players and posed uncertainty and possible disruption of traditional business models and led to an urgency to position the company also within this new digital landscape. The company's 1995 vision of reaching audiences, regardless of distribution channel and becoming a leading Scandinavian media company, aimed to give the company the compass to embark on its digital transformation and international expansion. However, Schibsted's plans for expansion were also a response to media ownership limits introduced in its home market, Norway. A range of initiatives were rapidly launched in the second half of the 1990s to begin the realization of the vision including establishing the first Scandinavian online portal, launching free newspapers in Europe, newspaper acquisitions in Sweden, the launch and development of online newspaper editions in Norway and Sweden, and the establishment of an online classified advertising site in Norway. However, its ambitious expansion that was financed by income from traditional print newspaper and television and film culminated in a major leadership crisis in the late 1990s, which was decisive for the future digital transformation and international expansion of the company.

However, around 1995, when the company's digital transformation and internationalization was initiated, this development was built on three factors, none of which was directly related to technology. First was the historical position of the company's newspapers in Norwegian society. Second was the ownership structure and form of the company. Third was the close relations and high levels of trust between the leadership figures of the company.

DOI: 10.4324/9781003439431-2

The Historical Position of Schibsted's Newspapers in Society

Schibsted started with the establishment of a book-printing press in 1839 by Christian Schibsted. To ensure regular printing, the company also began to publish a newspaper in 1860 that became *Aftenposten*, which was Norway's largest newspaper throughout the mid-twentieth century. Schibsted's acquisition of the Norwegian newspaper *Verdens Gang* (*VG*) in 1966 led to a dramatic expansion of the newspaper, and it became by far the largest newspaper in the country (Eide, 2008: 107). In fact, for decades, *VG* was the most distributed and sold newspaper in the Nordic region. This changed the company's standing. Schibsted's position as the owner of the two largest newspapers in Norway gave it a prominent position in its home market (Norland, 2001, 2011; Syvertsen et al., 2014: 102).

Throughout history, the printed press has had a key position in the formation of the Nordic region's countries as "open, democratic societies" (Syvertsen et al., 2014: 21). In fact, newspapers and their owners have traditionally provided "strong support for the view that media should appeal to all and should inform and enlighten the population at large, and consumption of newspapers has been high in all social groups" (Syvertsen et al., 2014). A further characteristic of the newspaper sector in the Nordic region is its "long and strong history of editorial freedom and well-functioning self-regulatory institutions" (Syvertsen et al., 2014: 21). Consequently, there have traditionally been more printed newspapers in the region when compared with other regions and countries.

The strength of the press in the region can partly be explained by the strong focus on education along with the emergence of political parties and parliamentarism in the region. While the British and US press and political parties were separate, "the voluntary collaboration and connections among newspapers and political parties in Scandinavia shaped the region's press structure. The party press came to play a key role as an 'agent of modernization,' contributing to democratization throughout the 1800s and 1900s" (Enli et al., 2018: 607).

While *Aftenposten* was published throughout World War II and faced penalties in the aftermath, its strong position remained (Norland, 2011; Syvertsen et al., 2014). *VG*, on the other hand, was originally tied to the Norwegian resistance movement during the war. The subscription-based newspaper, *Aftenposten*'s acquisition of the single-copy newspaper, *VG*, in 1966 was significant for the future Schibsted, as the agreement "came [with] a deep commitment to editorial independence and respect for the newspapers" (Norland, 2011: 278, author's translation).

The introduction of public newspaper subsidies in the region during the late 1960s and 1970s was key in shaping the region's industry further, and "the press became increasingly professionalized" (Enli et al., 2018: 611). Growth in advertising led to increased consolidation in the newspaper market, benefiting the

16 *Schibsted*

largest newspapers. Providing press subsidies to private newspapers were considered a cultural policy with the aim to support and uppold diversity on two levels: "diversity of political opinions and geographical diversity" throughout the region (Syvertsen et al., 2014: 54). Press subsidies were introduced in Norway in 1969, and later similar measures in Sweden, Finland and Denmark had been introduced by the early 1970s (Enli et al., 2018: 611; Syvertsen et al., 54). During the era of the party press system, *Aftenposten* was considered a conservative paper. Yet, in line with the "depolitization" and professionalization of newspapers, this political allegiance gradually faded. Increasingly, the editors' political outlooks varied from editor to editor (Norland, 2011: 209; Syvertsen et al., 2014: 101).

Most national newspapers in the region target large portions of the population. In contrast to the traditional divide between "Popular Press" and "Quality Press" in the United Kingdom, it is striking how the Norwegian press balance on a kind of "golden mean." For example, *VG* has been characterized as combining sensationalism and thoroughness (Eide, 2008: 168–169). Such a "middle-of-the-road" editorial approach is partly explained by the press subsidy measures and by smaller populations in the Nordic countries. Subsidies require national newspapers to avoid a "purely sensationalist" news approach, and they should address the entire population, not making distinctions between the more well-off and less well-off parts of the public. As such, the strong focus in the Nordic region on "universalism and egalitarianism is key to understanding the historical role of the newspaper sector within the Nordic welfare states" (Syvertsen et al., 2014: 57–58, Eide, 2008).

The Ownership Structure and Form

In the 1980s, the newspaper sector gradually moved from single-newspaper ownership to news companies that owned several newspapers. Until then, the *Aftenposten* owners' acquisition of *VG* in 1966 represented an exception, as owner concentration was an unfamiliar phenomenon in the news market in Norway, yet changes in ownership structure was to become "one of the most prominent features of the Norwegian newspaper landscape" (Hjeltnes, 2010: 421, author's translation). The Norwegian media sector looked toward international media trends and developments with interest. The fact that many US and other European newspapers were owned by large companies stimulated and "inspired to action also in this country as well" (Hjeltnes, 2010: 422, author's translation). The general turn toward a liberal ideology and deregulation of the Norwegian financial sector contributed to favorable conditions for adopting these trends (Hjeltnes, 2010: 422; Syvertsen et al., 2014). In 1985, Schibsted planned acquisitions of newspapers, publishers, and other media companies. In 1986, Aftenposten acquired shares in the subscription-based newspapers: Fædrelandsvennen in Kristiansand, Southern Norway and in Stavanger Aftenblad in Stavanger, Southwestern Norway, while VG acquired shares in Bladet Tromso in Tromso,

The Formation of the Modern Schibsted   17

Northern Norway and in Trondheim, Mid-Norway (Hjeltnes, 2010: 428). These initial investments would eventually lead to Schibsted fully acquiring and consolidating ownership of the three former newspapers around two decades later.

While Schibsted embarked on expansion through its wholly owned newspapers, the company simultaneously faced internal complications, as the company lacked leadership among the 17 family members with personal ownership (Hjeltnes, 2010: 437). The company's capital accumulation depended on the personal finances of the owners. Although not likely, if one of the owners went financially bankrupt, it could create financial problems for the company (Eide, 1995: 415). Kjell Aamot, CEO of *VG* from 1985 to 1989, was not happy with the situation and was determined to make changes: "Then, I had only one goal, and that was that *VG* had to become a limited company. . . . So, when we finally succeeded in doing so, I was looking forward to continuing in *VG*" (Aamot, interview with author, 2024). However, Aamot's success in turning *VG* into an independent joint-stock company meant that his days at *VG* were soon over. He was to become Schibsted's first CEO in 1989. However, while *VG* was solid financially, *Aftenposten* faced a dramatic decline in advertising revenue, and was facing major cost reductions and cuts (Norland, 2011: 291). The global management consultancy, McKinsey, was hired to advise the company, but it faced skepticism from representatives of the employees, who feared McKinsey's influence would mean "the end of the Schibstedianian spirit" (Norland, 2011: 291, author's translation).

Aftenposten's financial difficulties were only one of the problems for Schibsted, according to Birger Magnus, who worked at McKinsey and was the key consultant working with Schibsted from the late 1980s and into the 1990s. McKinsey's conclusion was to do two things, according to Magnus:

> One was restructuring in *Aftenposten*, and the other was the establishment of a Schibsted group model. We believed they had to establish a group that could follow up on the two companies: *Aftenposten* and *VG*. It could not just be the families that followed up. The companies needed a spearhead: the group model.
>
> (Magnus, interview with author, 2023)

Consequently, the management and owners decided on a new company structure and organization for Schibsted beyond 1987 and 1988, and the work "was further processed by the consulting firm McKinsey & Company" (Norland, 2011: 277, author's translation).

By then, Schibsted's media holdings included ownership of the national newspapers, *VG* and *Aftenposten*, Schibsted publishing, and co-ownership in several regional newspapers. Schibsted was established as a media group, but the competition between *VG* and *Aftenposten* as independent entities was strong and "repeated pushes to form common solutions were fruitless" (Norland, 2011:

18 *Schibsted*

278, author's translation). This was evident when Rolv Erik Ryssdal, hired by Schibsted in 1991, and future CEO of Schibsted (2009–2018), was tasked with exploring the possibilities for synergies within the newly integrated Schibsted:

> (Kjell) Aamot had started thinking about the group and integration, so he said to me that you can start looking at the possible synergy between *Aftenposten* and *VG*. It turned out that it was a rather unsuccessful project because they were not interested in talking to each other at all. I went around there and was called "The Synergist" and we laughed a lot about it later.
>
> (Ryssdal, interview with author, 2024)

Instead, the practice of individual subsidiaries competing continued within the Schibsted group, and this competitive dynamic came to characterize the future development of the company (Norland, 2011: 278). While the Schibsted group's board oversaw the company's portfolio of assets, the subsidiaries established their own boards with responsibility for the individual businesses (Norland, 2011: 286). Furthermore, McKinsey & Company had created a governance model for the company where the largest owner, Tinius Nagell-Erichsen, became the chairman of the board (Norland, 2011: 295).

While Schibsted had begun to make investmets in regional newspapers in 1986 (Hjeltnes, 2010: 428), now Schibsted was organized and was in a position to expand in a "unified direction as an industrial strategy" (Hjeltnes, 2010: 437, author's translation).

Two developments took place in 1992 that had major consequences for the future of Schibsted: the company launched TV2, the first national commercial television channel in Norway, and Schibsted was listed on the Norwegian stock exchange. In early 1991, the Norwegian Department of Culture invited applications for license to establish TV2, the first national advertising-funded television channel (Norland, 2011: 434). This represented a new threat to the Schibsted-owned *Aftenposten*'s advertising revenue. The newspaper was already in a severe financial situation with a loss of advertising revenue and a NOK 50 million deficit in the first quarter of 1990. The establishment of TV2 would have a big impact on the Norwegian advertising market, but it also represented a considerable opportunity for those controlling the new television channel. Therefore, Schibsted aimed at securing the TV2 license, thereby absorbing the competition and benefiting from the impact on the new television channel on the advertising market (Hjeltnes, 2010: 439).

Throughout the Spring 1991, Schibsted focused on developing plans for the TV2 proposal. Again, McKinsey was involved in Schibsted's corporate development. The CEO of Schibsted, Kjell Aamot, and chair of the *Aftenposten* board, Bjorn Atle Holter-Hovind, invited McKinsey to assess the opportunities TV2 represented for Schibsted. Senior consultants from McKinsey, including Birger Magnus, were central, and the consultancy's reports from similar projects internationally (i.e., RTL in Netherlands and Channel 4 in the United

The Formation of the Modern Schibsted   19

Kingdom) reportedly formed a basis for the work. McKinsey concluded that TV2 was an opportunity that had to be embraced by Schibsted (DN, 2001). The competitors for the TV2 license were the two largest news companies in Norway, Orkla and Schibsted. In November 1991, Schibsted won the license that included a ten-year national monopoly on terrestrial television advertising and a promise of an additional ten-year renewal (Norland, 2011: 435), and the year after TV2 was launched.

In 1992, Schibsted was listed on the Norwegian stock exchange. Tinius Nagell-Erichsen was originally against this listing – also called an IPO – because he feared outside investors and losing his position, but Ole Jacob Sunde, formerly at McKinsey Norway and an advisor to Nagell-Erichsen since the late 1980s, pointed out the strategic significance of the IPO for the company. While the company had been incorporated in 1989, it was still owned by the decedents of Christian Schibsted and there were constant conflicts stifling the business. "It was a tangle begging for a solution. The way out was listing the company" (Sunde, interview with author, 2024).

Sunde negotiated the terms and the Articles of Association prior to the IPO on behalf of Nagell-Erichsen, the largest Schibsted owner. The result became decisive for Schibsted's future, as Nagell-Erichsen held a controlling minority, which made it nearly impossible to take over the company without his consent: "As a listed company, Schibsted had the benefit of an anchor investor with a long-term perspective, while also being exposed to more impatient, agile shareholders with a shorter time horizon" (Sunde, interview with author, 2024). There were several layers of protection for Nagell-Erichsen, who owned 26.1 percent of the shares. Key among them was that no shareholder could own more than 30 percent of the shares, and changes in the Articles of Association required three-fourths majority at the company's general assembly (Norland, 2011: 297). As we shall see, Tinius Nagell-Erichsen's shareholdings would in 1996, be transferred to a trust named the Tinius Trust. Rolv Erik Ryssdal, involved in the work on the IPO at Schibsted, argues that the ownership combination has been decisive for Schibsted: "An IPO alone, without a long-term owner, would not have been good. The Trust has exercised wise, long-term ownership, while the stock listing has contributed to the necessary pace in relation to restructuring, transformation, and access to capital" (Ryssdal, interview with author, 2024). CEO of the Tinius Trust, Kristin Løken Stavrum, agrees, emphasizing how the Trust have aimed to ensure a willingness to take risks combined with long-term thinking (Løken Stavrum, interview with author, 2023).

The ideal of "the professional ownership," characterized by owners with a long-term perspective who respect editorial independence, contrasted with investors who first became aware of media investments in the 1980s and lacked such traditions and motives, became increasingly salient in media policy debates in Norway in the 1980s and 1990s. Schibsted was often highlighted as the "crown example" of such serious, professional ownership (Eide, 1995: 416). The new ownership structure and the stock listing were the key to the further development of the new Schibsted. Schibsted now entered a new era, and a

20 *Schibsted*

wave of expansion followed (Eide, 2008; Syvertsen et al., 2014: 102). Having invested horizontally in regional newspapers in the 1980s, now Schibsted continued to expand vertically and diagonally in film and television production companies. With the launch of the Schibsted co-owned TV2, the demand for television content increased, and Schibsted positioned itself in the value chain. In this way, Schibsted began to expand in an industrial fashion (Hjeltnes, 2010: 440). Still newspapers remained the cornerstone business. At that time in the early 1990s, the three largest news companies in Norway – Schibsted, Orkla, and A-pressen – together controlled 50 percent of the national newspaper circulation. Schibsted's wholly owned newspapers *Aftenposten* and *VG* alone controlled 30 percent of the total circulation (Eide, 1995: 419).

The Relations Within the Leadership Group

Scholars and journalists alike have drawn attention to the relationship between the first CEO of Schibsted, Kjell Aamot, and the company's largest owner, Tinius Nagell-Erichsen (Norland, 2011; Hjeltnes, 2010; Scholtz Nærø, 2005). This relation, as we shall see, was of great significance and proved to be key for the development of Schibsted. Nagell-Erichsen was considered an eccentric media owner, and Aamot points out how "Tinius was a special man. Both family members and others found him scary and where afraid of him" (Aamot, interview with author, 2024). Ole Jacob Sunde also describes Nagell-Erichsen as an unusual character, who he learned to approach in a specific manner:

> First, you had to give him new information first, to avoid him getting suspicious. Secondly, he wanted your candid opinion, without all the if's and but's. On the other hand, he could be sensitive to disapproving feedback and it would help to using humor and deliver it with a smile.
>
> (Sunde, interview with author, 2024)

CEO of Schibsted, Kjell Aamot, the senior executive at the company forging the closest relationship with Nagell-Erichsen, elaborates:

> I think the way I built trust was that, when we had a discussion, Tinius heard it in capital letters from me, while the others were partly afraid of him. He was confident in me because he knew that I said exactly what I meant, regardless of whether it was negative for him, so we had a very good relationship. He did have a bit of a fringe reputation, but when he acted in a bad way, it was mostly a form of personal insecurity. No harm was meant, but not everyone dared to stand up to him I did that.
>
> (Aamot, interview with author, 2024)

The management of the newly established Schibsted company consisted of only a handfull people. Anne Langbraaten, was one of the first hirees, joining Kjell Aamot from *VG*, as Finance manager. Later Langbraaten would work as director of finance and Chief Financial Officer (CFO) of Schibsted's first major online company until 2001. She thereby observed closely the development of the relationship between Aamot and Nagell-Erichsen from the very beginning, as well as the company's early digitization efforts:

> The fact that Kjell and Tinius had the relationship they had, and that Tinius had such great respect for Kjell, made this work. Otherwise, it would never have happened. Kjell was one of the few who managed to handle Tinius. I thought it was crucial. The relationship was very, very special. There are few who could handle Tinius the way Kjell could. That's probably what Kjell is good at. Kjell acknowledged the smaller things that Tinius was also concerned with, but at the same time managed to get the big thoughts planted.
>
> (Langbraaten, interview with author, 2024)

Tinius Nagell-Erichsen emphazises the mutual respect and solidity of the relationship:

> Kjell and I almost always disagree, but in a proper way and we both win in the end. We have never been enemies, even though the basis has been there. His way of being is reminiscent of a person pointing a gun at you and saying, please don't take it personally, but I'm going to pull the trigger. With Kjell you don't even see the gun.
>
> (Nagell-Erichsen quoted in Norland, 2011: 300, author's translation)

The relationship between Aamot and Nagell-Erichsen also proved vital for the successful recruitment of new senior executives and management and their ability to succeed within the company, and also the corporate culture emerging under Aamot's CEO reign:

> They trusted that I would give them the opportunity to do so, and then they gained confidence in that I had control over Tinus (Nagell-Erichsen). There were different people who worked well together, that is because I was a liberal. I knew nothing about these things (digitization), so I was completely dependent on them, and they were dependent on me. . . . My contribution was to keep the control over the board, but it was the others who knew how to do the job.
>
> (Aamot, interview with author, 2024)

The relationship between Kjell Aamot, Tinius Nagell-Erichsen, and key senior group executives was to be of major significance as Schibsted embarked on its digital transformation and international expansion.

The Multimedia and Internationalization Strategy and Vision

By 1995, Schibsted had around 2,200 employees, and that year the company's television and film operations generated NOK 1.5 billion, which was about half

22 *Schibsted*

of the company's revenue from printed media (Schibsted, 1995: 8; Hjeltnes, 2010: 442). TV2, in which Schibsted had a one-third ownership, was a huge financial success, earning profit three years after its launch in 1992 with NOK 1.2 billion in accumulated operating profits until the renewal of the license in 2002 (Norland, 2011: 435). In fact, by 1997, TV2 was the most profitable commercial television channel in Scandinavia (Schibsted, 1997: 4). Investments in TV and film continued, internationally, in Estonia in 1995, and in the Norwegian cable and satellite television channel, TVNorge, in 1996 (Schibsted, 1995, 1996).

However, despite major investments in TV and film, Schibsted, as a stock-listed company, experienced growing expectations from investors. This became increasingly evident when the CEO of Schibsted, Kjell Aamot, reported to the capital market in London and New York (Norland, 2011: 303). Already at the time of the stock listing, 20 percent of the company's shares was owned by international investors (Norland, 2011: 298). Investors asked why they should invest in Schibsted, and what the company's plans for growth and expansion were.

In 1994, Sverre Munck, was hired by Schibsted, as Executive Vice President (EVP), and was to have a key role in both the digitization and international expansion of the company for close to two decades. He had also experience from McKinsey. Munck points out that the expectations Schibsted experienced from the investors and international market were also tied to the fact that the company's newspapers still generated major revenues and profits:

> In the mid-1990s, all the number one print newspapers were still doing very well. They had strong cash flow – but as a newly listed company, Schibsted had to have another "equity story" beyond the strong cash flow: Why on earth should investors invest with us? We had to have a growth strategy.
>
> (Munck, interview with author, 2023)

Soon after Munck was appointed, he was presented with the opportunities of digitization and the Internet. During work on a new corporate strategy for Schibsted in the autumn of 1994, a representative from Goldman Sachs "spoke about browsers, networks and 'walled gardens' such as Prodigy and AOL," Munck recalls (Munck, interview with author, 2023). Throughout the winter of 1994–1995, at a time when not even Microsoft had an Internet strategy in place, there was a growing awareness and consciousness within Schibsted group's senior management of Internet's significance for media (Norland, 2011: 304).

Birger Magnus, then partner in McKinsey Norway, and involved in Schibsted as a management consultant since the late 1980s, also came to play a key role in the digitization and internationalization of Schibsted: "McKinsey was hired by Schibsted, and when the McKinsey team with Birger Magnus came and outlined developments, opportunities and possible strategic moves, it opens a big world, and you must figure out how to navigate" (Langbraaten, interview with author, 2024).

The Formation of the Modern Schibsted   23

Several important steps and decisions were made around 1995 that would anchor Schibsted's goals for digital transformation and international expansion. McKinsey, with Birger Magnus, advised the company to internationalize and becoming Scandinavian as well as aiming to reach customers regardless of distribution channel. In fact, this advice was to become the new vision of the company: "Schibsted's ambition is to become Scandinavia's leading media company through being the preferred supplier of content to readers, viewers and advertisers, irrespective of their choice of media" (Schibsted, 1995). As Birger Magnus remarks, the vision was "[a] very simple sentence, which Kjell (Aamot, the CEO of Schibsted) thought was very expensive. He had to pay an entire McKinsey team to get it" (Magnus, interview with author, 2024).

In the wake of these developments, Birger Magnus was hired by Schibsted as Deputy CEO of Schibsted and Executive Vice President of News in 1996 and worked at Schibsted until 2009. Schibsted's relationship with McKinsey was to continue throughout the digital transformation and international expansion, either in the form of consultancy or by hiring McKinsey consultants that have been working close with Schibsted or people with a general McKinsey background. The significance of the close relations was underlined by Kjell Aamot, CEO of Schibsted: "McKinsey represents access to an important network. To have McKinsey as an element in the leadership group, is important" (Aamot quoted in DN, 2001, author's translation).

The new *Multimedia division*, established in 1995, was the key to realizing the new strategic vision along with the established *Print Media* and *TV/Film* divisions (Schibsted, 1995). Schibsted now moved from being a newspaper company to a media group, with traditional newspapers as the core business, but with expansion into the television and film sector and early moves into electronic media (Schibsted, 1995).

During the second half of the 1990s, Schibsted's initial operationalization of the company's new vision happened at breathtaking pace and scope through vertical, horizontal, and diagonal acquisitions and expansions, all taking place under Kjell Aamot's reign and the newly appointed members of the leader group. Aleksander Rosinski, first hired as a Schibsted trainee in 2000, with numerous management and board roles across the Schibsted group until today, argues that the management style and the relations between senior management in this formative period, of the digital and international Schibsted, set it apart from other companies:

A starting point for how I think about the beginning of Schibsted's digital transformation is that all media managers around 1993, 1994, 1995 had access to more or less the same information, but still made different decisions. There are many reasons for why different decisions were made, but to try to understand why Schibsted made radically different decisions compared to almost all other media companies that had roughly the same starting

24 *Schibsted*

point, i.e. classic media conglomerates, which owned newspapers, film, TV and radio, I think a decisive factor is how Schibsted's group management was composed, the dynamic between them and how they worked together. At the time, this group of people consisted mainly of Birger Magnus, Kjell Aamot and Sverre Munck, but also to some extent Tinius Nagell-Erichsen, and some other central people.

(Rosinski, interview with author, 2024)

The major corporate initiatives aimed at realizing Schibsted's vision of 1995 of digital and international expansion in the second half of the 1990s, included the establishment of a Scandinavian online portal, newspaper acquisitions in Sweden, the launch and development of online newspaper editions in Norway and Sweden, a pioneering online classified advertising site, the expansion of free newspapers in Europe, and a company-wide management trainee program, together with the establishment of the Tinius Trust as the controlling owner, that aimed to secure stability and long-term thinking in terms of Schibsted's development. However, Schibsted's expansion outside Norway should also be seen in light of the national limits to media ownership introduced in 1997. Due to growing fears of reduced media pluralism and to safeguard freedom of expression, and to limit particularly Schibsted's domestic expansion, media ownership was set to a maximum one-third of any specific market (Syvertsen, 2004; Syvertsen et al., 2014: 104).

Scandinavia Online

The Amandus project, headed by the Schibsted newspaper, *Aftenposten*'s CEO Kåre Frydenlund and Birger Magnus and Birger Steen at McKinsey Norway, took place in the spring of 1995. The outcome was a business plan and outline for Schibsted's first major multimedia investment: an Internet portal reminiscent of American Online. Internationally, and particularly in the United States, Internet portals were seen as the best way to attract and capitalize on the growing number of Internet users. There was uncertainty as to how successful legacy newspapers would be online, and Internet portals were considered a platform for news as well. The portal would be the key to the first stage of realizing the new vision that McKinsey had already created:

The background for this portal was that we as consultants in 1994–1995 created the vision of Schibsted going digital and going international. And, we said that the first step should be to create an online service. . . . We concluded that such an online service should be built. This is the future.

(Magnus, interview with author, 2024)

The Internet portal would be a proactive response to the possible disruptive effects of the Internet (Schibsted, 1996: 4) but also aimed to protect against

The Formation of the Modern Schibsted 25

competition from expanding US online portals by upholding Schibsted's principles of avoiding gatekeepers in the digital domain, Munck points out:

> We were courted – I don't remember if it was by Prodigy or America Online –and they wanted exclusive access to our readers in exchange for us getting preferred placement and presumably some payment. But, quite early on we decided that no, we're not going to have a "gatekeeper" between us and our readers and advertisers. And this awareness of the role of potential gatekeepers – both in relation to readers and advertisers – is a dimension that has characterized Schibsted all along, while I was there and to this very day.
>
> (Munck, interview with author, 2023)

Schibsted's *Multimedia* unit was established in 1995 and shortly after bought OsloNett. The company had two main business areas:

> [A]n ISP business, and a media part which contained, among other things, the search engine Kvasir, a directory like Yahoo! and some pure media content, which were called "home pages" at the time. OsloNett was immediately renamed Schibsted Nett with the domain www.sn.no.
>
> (Munck, interview with author, 2023)

The Internet was still in its infancy, and Birger Magnus recalls when Schibsted acquired Kvasir, online search was still not seen as the major business opportunity it later developed into:

> [T]he Kvasir search engine was actually very advanced, and if we had gone international with it, we (Schibsted) would have become very rich. We didn't see the potential in Kvasir, at the time. It was long before Google, although Yahoo! was beginning to emerge.
>
> (Magnus, interview with author, 2023)

In fact, Munck remembers how, at the time, a large US Internet company contacted Schibsted wishing to acquire or license the technology of the search engine, Kvasir, but again Schibsted emphasized its strategy to become digital and leading in Scandinavia and not contribute to the international expansion of foreign companies into the region (Munck, interview with author, 2023).

Toward the end of 1996, Schibsted decided to move out of telecom, to concentrate on the Internet portal, as Telenor, the former Norwegian state telecom, agreed to acquire Schibsted Nett's access operation. Then, in January 1997, the Internet portal or "gateway company" *Scandinavia Online* (SOL) was established as a joint venture between Schibsted (65 percent) and Telenor (35 percent) with 50/50 voting control. The new company aimed to become "the dominating Online channel in Norway and Scandinavia" (Schibsted, 1996: 6). Torry Pedersen, former Chief Editor and CEO of *VG*, argues, "[T]here was

26 *Schibsted*

an incredible amount of experimentation, and everyone was supposed to have their own portal at the time, but *Scandinavia Online* was of course the big and dominant one" (Pedersen, interview with author, 2023). By 1997, Schibsted's "principal activities in the Internet are channeled through *Scandinavia Online*" (Schibsted Annual Report, 1996: 6). Birger Magnus underlines this belief:

> [T]hen we thought that such a portal was the future, and that all media content was to be distributed through it. At least until 1997/1998, we thought that this was the way ahead.
>
> (Magnus, interview with author, 2024)

Schibsted's two largest newspapers, the Swedish *Aftonbladet* and *VG* in Norway also had to contribute with content.

The Tinius Trust

In 1996, Schibsted's largest shareholder Tinius Nagell-Erichsen, formed the Tinius Trust (Stiftelsen Tinius) (Schibsted, 1996). Ole Jacob Sunde, close financial advisor to Tinius Nagell-Eriksen since the late 1980s, became the board member of the Trust in 1996, and later the chair of the board when Nagell-Erichsen passed away in 2007. Sunde also became the board member of Schibsted in 2000, and the Chair of the board of Schibsted (2002–2022). At first, Nagell-Erichsen's holdings were organized in the company Blommenholm. Sunde points out:

> In hindsight, throughout the 1990s we lay the foundation for the decennials to follow. We moved Tinius' shares to an investment company, Blommenholm Industrier AS, in 1994 to be able vote for the combined power of 26.1% exceeding the 25% threshold in the articles of association.
>
> (Sunde, interview with author, 2024)

In 1996, these holdings were then transferred into the Tinius Trust. Sunde points out that this relates to his problematic relations with his inheritors:

> Two years later, the Tinius Trust was established with the aim of taking control of the golden shares of Blommenholm Industrier when Mr. Nagell-Erichsen passed away. He did not believe that his children had experience nor interest to upholding the ownership in his spirit. Rather he entrusted the power to a board of three, "being the best he could find."
>
> (Sunde, interview with author, 2024)

The members of the Trust's board were Ole Jacob Sunde, John Rein, and Bjorn A. Holter-Hovind, with Tinius Nagell-Erichsen as the chairman. "Why these persons? We have worked together for many years in the reorganization of

The Formation of the Modern Schibsted   27

Schibsted. They have knowledge of the Group's business affairs, and I know no one better," Nagell-Erichsen underlined (Schibsted, 1996). The Trust was formed to ensure that the Schibsted group would remain a media group, operating according to the editorial and business guidelines and to secure the future of the company in accordance with the Articles of Association. Sunde points out the significance of organizing Nagell-Erichsen's holdings in this way for the development of Schibsted: The company's structure accommodates both the more aggressive, short-term, flexible and profit-seeking motive of the stock market, but its largest owner, the Tinius Trust, represented the opposite. Together, this created a dynamic that has been the key for the success of Schibsted:

> In a listed company, the board of directors would often find it challenging to take a long-term view. However, with backing from a trust, which in its character is perpetual, the board will be able to counter this inclination. This creates a different atmosphere in the boardroom. The directors' willingness to take on risk when allocating capital increase.
>
> (Sunde, interview with author, 2024)

The establishment of the Tinius Trust, then, was to secure a long-term view on Schibsted's development, a view that also defined value development beyond quarterly reports and the stock market, the current CEO of the Tinius Trust, Kristin Løken Stavrum, argues (Løken Stavrum, interview with author, 2023).

Aftonbladet and Svenska Dagbladet

In 1996, the acquisition of 49.9 percent of the Swedish newspaper *Aftonbladet*, a single-copy print newspaper founded in 1930 from the Swedish Trade Union Confederation, marked the beginning of Schibsted's transformation into a Scandinavian company. Later, Schibsted would increase its ownershare to over 90 percent, with the trade union retaining a minority share (Benson, et al., 2025). However, through its initial ownership share, Schibsted took the business and economic responsibility of the newspaper. The aquisition was also of major strategic importance. Rolv Erik Ryssdal, the second CEO of Schibsted (2009–2018) and installed as CEO of *Aftonbladet in* 1996, elaborates:

> Schibsted, like many other Norwegian companies, when they wanted to internationalize, they often go to Sweden. We had bought some TV stations and such in Estonia earlier, but the big acquisition was the Swedish newspaper, *Aftonbladet.* Since it was such a strong and powerful organization with a continuing, very important and strong growth and development, it in effect provided a bridgehead into Sweden that gave us the position and opportunity to do the other things that we later did in Sweden. So, beyond the fact that *Aftonbladet* was bought, that transaction turned out to be enormously strategically important. Gunnar Stromblad played a key role, clearly

28 *Schibsted*

in *Aftonbladet*, but later in Schibsted in Sweden, and the entire Schibsted group.

(Ryssdal, interview with author, 2024)

In 1996, *Aftonbladet*'s circulation surpassed *Expressen*'s, and thereby became the largest newspaper in Sweden. The same year, *Aftonbladet* was the first Swedish newspaper with an Internet edition. Throughout the year, its online edition developed into a complete electronic newspaper. The number of visitors rose quickly, reaching one million by the end of the year 1996, and it was the most frequently visited online newspaper in Sweden (Schibsted, 1996: 37).

The same year, Birger Magnus had been appointed as Schibsted's Deputy CEO and EVP for News. In this new position, he became one of the key members of the group's leadership, responsible for realizing the company's vision that he had been central in developing as a McKinsey consultant. "Then I had been hired in the number two position at Schibsted and we had the mandate to go international and go digital. Those were actually two things we weren't," Magnus recalls (Magnus, interview with author, 2023). Magnus was also installed as the chairman of *Aftonbladet*, following Schibsted's acquisition of the newspaper which proved to be decisive for Schibsted's expansion:

> For me, *Aftonbladet* was crucial. It was difficult to become a prophet in one's own country (Norway). Although I got along very well with the people in *VG*, I couldn't tell *VG* what do in relation to digitization and the expanding Internet. However, when I could point to *Aftonbladet*'s pioneering and exciting online initiatives, it forced a competition between the two organizations. This made my role much easier. Without *Aftonbladet* and its culture, which was full of commitment and energy, and which was to take on the competition with *Expressen* and Bonnier, and succeeded in a fantastic way, it would have been more difficult. *VG* had lots of energy, but *Aftonbladet* had a faster pace and greater urge to explore. However, such dynamics are often difficult to see and understand from the outside, and I didn't understand it either until it happened: 'Wow, here you've got a tool and something you can use that is worth its weight in gold,' I thought.
>
> (Magnus, interview with author, 2024)

The acquisition of *Aftonbladet*, that was to become the largest newspaper in Sweden, had several benefits for Schibsted. The newspaper had a strong innovative culture and it was ahead in its online development, and it was important for the Schibsted group in a wider sense as *VG* and *Aftonbladet* could learn from each other (Magnus, interview with author, 2024).

In Sweden, *Aftonbladet*'s financial results for 1998 were the best ever. Income from advertising increased and the newspaper's market share for sales was the highest in modern times. *Aftonbladet*'s Internet offerings continued to be superior in Sweden and contributed positively to the financial results (Schibsted, 1998: 32). In Norway, the circulation of newspapers had stabilized at high levels, but the newspaper market in the country did not have the continuous growth as it has had earlier. Still, newspaper consumption in the country remained at the top internationally, even while the emergence of new media services were increasing and the competition for readers was intensifying (Schibsted, 1998: 32). Then, in 1998, Schibsted acquired 73.6 percent of *Svenska Dagbladet*, a subscription-based newspaper and one of the leading papers in Sweden, making the company a considerable newspaper player in Sweden and a major Nordic newspaper company (Syvertsen et al., 2014: 100). Schibsted would later take full ownership of *Svenska Dagbladet* turning Schibsted into one of the major newspaper owners in Sweden.

Online Newspaper Editions

When the Schibsted-owned newspaper, *VG*, launched its first online edition in 1995, it was a small initiative. Former Chief Editor and CEO of *VG*, Torry Pedersen, explains: "When *VG* came online in 1995, there were literally 3–4 people sitting under the stairs. It was relatively miserable conditions they worked under" (Pedersen, interview with author 2023). In Sweden, *Aftonbladet* was the first Swedish newspaper to launch an online version, and it developed into a complete digital newspaper version throughout 1996 (Schibsted, 1996: 37). By, 1998, *Aftonbladet* was the largest news outlet online in Sweden. With 200,000 daily visitors, the newspaper was roughly three times larger than its closest competitor. No other newspaper in Europe had as many daily readers online (Schibsted, 1998: 33). The same year, the Norwegian newspaper, *VG*, became Norway's most-visited online newspaper. The number of users increased throughout the year, and by the end of the year, it had 130,000 daily readers (Schibsted, 1998: 31). In fact, overall, the number of online newspapers in Norway grew rapidly from 17 in 1995 to 120 in 1997 (Krumsvik, 2006: 284). Despite great financial results in 1998, Schibsted forecast a challenging future for the print edition of *Aftonbladet*, which demanded a change in course. The print newspaper existed within a shrinking market, which called for a change in strategic direction. The progress seen in the 1990s was largely the result of its core activity: sales of *Aftonbladet* copies, but in the latter years, as online services emerged and made great progress, the newspaper was changing and expanding to becoming a media house. Schibsted argued that the core of traditional newspaper was well suited for digital media, and *Aftonbladet*'s staff had a unique competence (Schibsted, 1998). By 1999, Schibsted's Norwegian and Swedish online newspapers had strengthened their market positions and had become among the most-visited online sites in these countries (Schibsted, 1999: 15).

Free Newspapers Internationally

The print newspapers began to launch online editions in the second half of the 1990s to position themselves and prepare for competition within the expanding

30 *Schibsted*

online domain. However, at the same time, a print newspaper business model emerged that represented both new competition, but also an opportunity for Schibsted. The free newspaper, *Metro*, was launched in Sweden by the Nordic media company, Modern Times Group, in 1995. *Metro* turned a profit in its first year and became the most read morning newspaper in Sweden. *Metro* was then launched internationally in Europe, the United States, and Canada in 1999 and 2000 (Anand and Hood, 2007: 12). While the acquisition of *Aftonbladet* and *Svenska Dagbladet* was key to turning Schibsted into a Scandinavian company, the company's decission to launch free newspapers internationally signaled an ambition to go beyond the region with its core business area. In 1999, Schibsted launched free newspapers in Norway, Germany, and Switzerland. The newspaper, *Avis1*, was published every Wednesday in Oslo, Norway, with a circulation of around 200,000, and the free newspaper, *20 Minutes*, was launched in Cologne, Germany, and Zurich, Switzerland. The latter became the second most read newspaper in Zurich with 310,000 daily readers. However, in Cologne, local newspaper publishers attempted to stop the publication of *20 Minutes* through the courts, but the ruling was in favor of Schibsted, who continued to publish (Schibsted, 1999: 15). The year after, in 2000, *20 Minutes* was launched in Spain and France. The free newspaper business model demanded lower costs since it did not run a subscription operation, its income relied entirely on advertising, it was published in tabloid format, and its production required a much smaller staff since it relied more on wire content and news agencies compared to traditional newspaper (Anand and Hood, 2007: 13).

Classified Advertising Online

By 1999, Schibsted's newspaper ownership in Norway included the wholly owned national *VG* and *Aftenposten*, and a 32 percent ownership share in *Adresseavisen*, 31 percent in Stavanger *Aftenblad*, 24 percent in *Bergens Tidende*, and 25 percent in *Fædrelandsvennen* (Schibsted, 1999: 9). The three former regional newspapers' collaboration in print advertising sales and distribution throughout the 1990s, with *Fædrelandsvennen* joining later, proved decisive for the newspapers' coming joint efforts to expand into online classified advertising (Munch, interview with author, 2024). There was a growing awareness of the effect of the Internet on its classified advertisements within Schibsted, but also the possibilities for the company, Sverre Munck says:

> In the beginning we focused very much on online news, but we also had a realization around 1996, maybe 1997, which we later put a name to it, in fact it became a mantra for us: "The Internet is made for classified, and classifieds are made for the Internet." We realized that the functionality that the Internet enabled was going to be infinitely better than what was possible on

The Formation of the Modern Schibsted 31

paper. It turned into the dominant technology for classified advertising. We were probably not aware of all the positive implications of the Internet, but we did see the possibilities.

(Munck, interview with author, 2023)

The early collaboration between regional newspapers in which Schibsted had ownership shares was important, as there was a mutual interest in exploring possibilities online. In 1999, the joint experimental online classified advertising site *vis@avisen* was launched. The site published PDF versions of the print classified advertisement online. Didrik Munch, then CEO of *Bergens Tidende*, explains:

> It was the regional newspapers, *Adresseavisen, Bergens Tidende, Stavanger Aftenblad*, that primarily worked on this project. *Vis@avisen*, the precursor to FINN. We figured we had to test it out. It was, after all, showing the print ads in PDF format online.
>
> (Munch, interview with author 2024)

However, the pioneering move into online classified advertising was limited and quite basic. The site was not a success, and other competing sites for jobs and real estate advertising were growing and establishing leading market positions. Still, this early initiative proved to be very important for Schibsted's expansion into online classified advertising (Anand and Hood, 2007: 9). Terje Seljeseth, head of IT at the national newspaper, *Aftenposten*, was the only technically adept person in the leadership group of the newspaper. Seljeseth was aware of how online developments could be a threat to classified advertising, not only for *Aftenposten* but also for the regional newspapers:

> I was part of the leadership group at *Aftenposten* in 1998, 1999. Then, the Internet started to show its face. What was very clear in *Aftenposten*, but also in the regional newspapers, which *Aftenposten* collaborated with was that the internet could quickly pose a threat to classified ads. They made up a significant part of *Aftenposten*'s total income. At least several tens of percents of the total income. So, if there were to be a sudden change in that, it would be quite a big threat for *Aftenposten* and other classified advertising carrying newspapers. It became an increasingly frequent part of the strategy discussion in the leadership group in *Aftenposten*.
>
> (Seljeseth, interview with author, 2024)

These discussions led to the establishment of the online classified company, FINN, in 1999–2000, headed by Seljeseth, which was to disrupt the classified business in Norway and spurred Schibsted's major classified expansion internationally.

32 *Schibsted*

Schibsted's Amandus Trainee Program

The vision formulated in 1995 underlined how Schibsted should develop into "Scandinavia's leading media company." The company defined "leading" by not only focusing on market shares and positions, but also in terms of becoming "the most attractive company for the best qualified employees" (Schibsted, 1996: 6–7). At the end of 1996, the number of employees in the group was 2,530, of which 500 were employed outside Norway. Due to acquisitions of new companies, the number of employees abroad had increased by approximately 400 in 1996. The group's rapid growth and expansion necessitated the transfer of employees between companies. A key priority was therefore the systemization of this work (Schibsted, 1996).

Schibsted aimed to become the "Scandinavia's leading media company" through focusing on developing competency and quality at management level. This would give the company a competitive advantage, which would lead to growth (Schibsted, 1996: 4). The key iniative was the launch in January 1997 of a two-year trainee program, *Amandus*, initiated by Birger Magnus and Birger Steen (Norland, 2011: 326) . The acquisition of a large company such as *Aftonbladet* in 1996 contributed to supporting this initiative and exemplified how to realize this part of the Schibsted vision:

> The acquisition of *Aftonbladet* gave us more legs to stand on, and this gave the trainees and the company more opportunities. The company wasn't just a monolith. There were now several subsidiaries to play on, and which could also learn from each other.
>
> (Magnus, interview with author, 2024)

During the programme's first two years, the trainees had four different postings in subsidiaries, within four major business areas. By 1999, 28 trainees had completed the programme, and most of them had accepted positions within Schibsted (Schibsted, 1999).

Rebellion and Leadership Crises

These major initiatives in the second half of the 1990s represented the formative phase of the realization of Schibsted's 1995 vision of digital transformation and international expansion. However, the combination of the company's aggressive expansion, major investments, and risk-taking culminated in fierce criticism of Kjell Aamot, the CEO of Schibsted. There were disagreements as to how the company was being run. During the two years leading up to the rebellion in 1999, a growing unease in parts of the Schibsted board had developed over the proliferation of new initiatives and ventures and their financial costs (Norland, 2011). Already when Schibsted's Multimedia division was established in 1996, Sverre Munck reflects on the emerging challenges with digital investments:

> I was the Chief Financial Officer at Schibsted at the time and had to explain to the shareholders what we were going to spend the money on. And we realized quite early on that the digital had a completely different risk profile – and a completely different investment horizon – than our print newspapers had, which at the time were still money machines.
>
> (Munck, interview with author, 2023)

Investments in the development and digital products and services differed from traditional acquisitions and investments; Ole Jacob Sunde, explains:

> Digitalization is expensive. Listed companies are valued as a multiple of earnings, making digitalization through organic growth less attractive. While the cost of acquisitions is booked as an investment in the balance sheet, organic development will burden the bottom line since it requires more employees and increased marketing and the associated revenues from these expenses will come two, three years later at best.
>
> (Sunde, interview with author, 2024)

Several of the board members came from traditional industries such as forrestry and shipping and were new to the logic and risks associated with Internet investments and digital expansion; Birger Magnus, argues:

> [I]f you look at the composition of the board of the Schibsted group, there were many members with a background in traditional industry. It was Jan Reinås (forestry). It was Einar Kloster (shipping). Bjørn Atle Holter-Hovind had helped start TV2, so he was perhaps a bit of an exception, but most of them had a more industrial background. They were not used to the logic of the Internet economy. You had to invest a lot upfront, before you could reap the benefits from the network effects, of which FINN, was a key example.
>
> (Magnus, interview with author, 2024)

Bjørn Atle Holter-Hovind, the Schibsted board member who represented the largest and powerful shareholder, Tinis Nagell-Erichsen, was worried and wanted to remove Kjell Aamot. Ole Jacob Sunde explains:

> There was a mounting uneasiness among the management, board and the main owner toward the end of the 1990s. The results were deteriorating in the wake of acquisitions in Sweden and the dot-com crisis in 2000. Particularly, *Svenska Dagbladet*, was underperforming. Bjørn-Atle Holter Hovind,

34 *Schibsted*

who represented Tinius at the board, was concerned and suggested a change of CEO.

(Sunde, interview with author, 2024)

While pointing out the strengths of Aamot's management style, Magnus also acknowledges how the Schibsted management could be perceived as operating with levels of risk that were too high. From the perspective of the Schibsted board, there was reason to be doubtful and, at the same time, some in management were also a little skeptical about Aamot's style of leadership:

> Kjell Aamot was a very good communicator, particularly in relation to the board and the owners. However, he was perhaps not the kind of CEO who led the businesses and the organization systematically. We were given pretty much free rein – in good and bad. The good thing was that he motivated talented employees to innovate. However, we could probably have had a clearer governance and, among other things, better control over costs. From the Schibsted group board's point of view, we could appear to be very forward-leaning, but sometimes a bit "fast" and taking a bit too much risk. At the time, in addition to all the digital products, we launched the commuter newspaper *20 Minutes* in Switzerland and Germany in December 1999. In addition, the Swedish newspaper *Svenska Dagbladet* had major financial problems. When the capital market naturally reacted, it was necessary for the board of the group to ask: 'How do we get through this?'

(Magnus, interview with author, 2024)

Others argue that it was external factors that caused the unrest. In the end, Aamot was allowed to stay, largely because Tinius chose it, but it also showed how close Aamot and Tinius's relationship was:

> Tinius asked for my advice. In my view the lacking performance was a result of market factors rather than mismanagement. For Tinius, there was also another aspect. Kjell was one of the few people he trusted. They were very close, somewhat of a symbiosis, and this close relationship would be important to take the steps necessary to solve the challenges. So, I advised against firing Kjell.

(Sunde, interview with author, 2024)

The relationship between them, and the way Aamot was able to handle Nagell-Erichsen was crucial for the development of Schibsted, Magnus argues:

> The board was skeptical about Kjell, but Tinius put his protective hand over him. Tinius was a very special person, and Kjell's great strength was that he managed to handle Tinius and had his full trust. Kjell was very socially

The Formation of the Modern Schibsted   35

intelligent, and was fantastic at handling people, especially Tinius. Their mutual dependence after the discussions in the board became even greater.
(Magnus, interview with author, 2024)

Through his relationship with Kjell Aamot, Tinius Nagell-Erichsen, the main shareholder, believed that he exerted the greatest influence over the company, and without Aamot, he would not feel safe (Norland, 2011: 322). While Aamot stayed, Bjørn-Atle Holter Hovind left the Schibsted board and Ole Jacob Sunde replaced him as representative of Tinius Nagell-Erichsen in 2002. Schibsted steered through the leadership crises, but a new major crisis was on the horizon.

Conclusion

The modernization of Schibsted and its pioneering strategies for digital and international expansion and operationalization of them was shaped by the dynamic between centralization and decentralization in various ways (Noam, 2019). The dynamic can be explained
by the combination of the external dimensions, company dimensions, and leadership dimensions.

In terms of external dimensions, traditionally Schibsted's newspapers have shaped, but also been shaped, by the region's media system and society. The company wished to extend its strong position in the Norwegian, and later Swedish media markets, and into the emerging digital domain in the mid-1990s. Schibsted aimed to continue serving as a cornerstone institution and bulwark from international competition in the region.

In terms of the company dimensions, already around 1990s, after the Schibsted group was formed, there were attempts to create synergies between its two main media assets, the newspapers *VG* and *Aftenposten*. These early attempts were unsuccesful, yet it was an indicator of how Schibsted and its newspapers would seek synergies, while continuing to compete, in the future. In the wake of the listing of Schibsted, the ownership structure meant that the Tinius Trust had negative control and offered a long-term perspective for the company, as well as protection against takeover by investors. Yet the company was also exposed to the stock market and international investors. This ownership structure created a dynamic that was to shape the company throughout its digital and international expansion.

Increased competition for advertising and a maturing, commercial media sector, coupled with expectations from investors and growth ambitions, as well as the introduction of limits to media ownership in Norway, led to the traditional newspaper company expanding diagonally and vertically into television and film, and horizontally with the acquisition of the Swedish *Aftonbladet* and *Svenska Dagbladet* in 1996 and 1998, respectively. The early expansion into multimedia in the mid-1990s was also a response to investors' and the company's growth ambitions, aiming to position the company in the digital domain, addressing both the potential opportunities and challenges to traditional media and advertising business models.

36 *Schibsted*

Already in this early digital phase, the relationship between centralization and decentralization became an issue. Schibsted centrally initiated the creation of the Internet portal, *Scandinavia Online*, in 1996. Internationally, US Internet companies considered portals the key to connecting media content and services with the growing number of online users. Schibsted aimed be an early adopter in Scandinavia and rapidly establish a dominant position for the portal, becoming competitive against internationally expanding companies in the emerging regional digital market. The portal also aligned with the corporate policy of avoiding gatekeepers and intermediaries, while not losing control of the connection between its media content and audience, which was the key to generating advertising revenue and sales. Yet parallel to this central Internet portal initiative, Schibsted's wholly and partly owned newspapers collaborated to create Schibsted's first online classified advertising service in the late 1990s. This was initiated by the newspapers themselves, yet supported by Schibsted centrally, highlighting also the decentralized character of Schibsted and the autonomy of the individual newspapers.

The leadership dimension played a significant role in the modernization of Schibsted and its early digital expansion, especially in relation to two key aspects. First, the CEO of Schibsted, Kjell Aamot, sought to balance Schibsted's central initiatives with the autonomy of the newspapers, but he gave senior management freedom to pursue the company's early digital inititatives. As such, Aamot's role as confidant of the largest shareholder, Tinius Nagell-Erichsen, and the mutual trust between them, was key to moving the company into the digital era. In this sense, digitization initiatives required a new type of manager, who focused on a wider set of tasks and issues, including digital innovation and the risks involved when expanding into the digital domain (Artero and Manfredi, 2016). The combination of Aamot's risk-taking, lax, and trust-based management style also meant that he was open to criticism from Schibsted's board and investors, who questioned his style of running the company. Yet, to some degree, this was also because the board lacked the competence to understand the business logics of the digital transformation, as several came from other traditional industries. Second, a striking aspect in terms of leadership is the close relation between the Schibsted senior management and the global management consultancy McKinsey. McKinsey played a central role in major corporate strategy decisions and how they were implemented, including the ownership structure, the expansion into television channel ownership, the development of the first multimedia strategy, and the decision to build the Internet portal, *Scandinavia Online*. Birger Magnus and Sverre Munck, together with CEO Kjell Aamot, were the most influential Schibsted executives in the leadership group from this early phase and throughout the digital transformation and international expansion until the late 2000s, both had McKinsey background. So, had Ole Jacob Sunde, the financial advisor of Tinius Nagell-Erichsen since the 1980s and later the chairman of both Schibsted and the Tinius Trust. Magnus was the key McKinsey consultant when the consultancy worked with Schibsted from the late 1980s until he was hired by the company in 1996. The close connection meant that Schibsted was continually exposed to and shaped by the strategies and tools derived from the US media and burgeoning Internet industry that were the central drivers of the digital transformation worldwide. Kjell Aamot, the first CEO of Schibsted, stated that having McKinsey as "an element" in the leadership of Schibsted was important, among others, as it gave access to a significant network (DN, 2001). The close relationship between Schibsted and McKinsey draws attention to how companies may form a certain dependency on management consultancies, in a cycle of promoting and selling advice and implementation, particularly in the face of uncertainty of digitization (McKenna, 2012).

3 The Emergence of the Digital and International Schibsted

2000–2009

The Dot-com crash, combined with the earlier leadership crises, impacted severely on Schibsted. The company's group management needed to regain the board's trust and was expected to reduce its investments and made major divestments. However, Schibsted was also allowed to continue its Internet investments, although more carefully and considerate. This proved decisive for the company's future. Schibsted differed from many other media companies who reduced or stopped Internet investments in the wake of the dot-com crash. This combination gave Schibsted the momentum and a competitive advantage in the digital transformation of its media houses and classified advertising and the international expansion of the latter that this chapter details. Still, Schibsted's digital expansion in the 2000s also faced criticism and was seen as controversial and of high risk. The search for digital business models and organizational changes to meet digitization and expand internationally increasingly challenged the traditional ways of running newspapers, advertising operations, and a national media organization. Launched only two days after the dot-com bubble burst, the company's pioneering online classified operation in Norway, FINN, soon proved to be a major success and spurred the rapid international expansion of online classified advertising sites in this period. Yet, FINN was controversial as it cannibalized the company's print newspapers' classified operations. Consolidation within its news business to remain competitive in the emerging digital market raised fears of market dominance and loss of media diversity and created conflict within the Schibsted's leadership. And, despite a more restrictive approach to Internet investments, in the mid-2000s, Schibsted went head to head with the emerging global platforms launching an ambitious, high-risk, and costly regional online search engine, as well as a social media service. Still, by 2007, Schibsted reported record profits, of which 51 percent came from its online businesses. Then, the financial crisis hit the world economy, with major consequences for the company.

The Dot-Com Crash and Schibsted

In March 2000, the "Dot-com bubble" burst, as the value of Internet investments plummeted across the world, with major consequences also for

DOI: 10.4324/9781003439431-3

The Emergence of the Digital and International Schibsted   39

media companies, including Schibsted. Schibsted's stock value decreased with 65 percent by December 2000. Throughout 2001, Schibsted lost NOK 350 million, and the main losses were in *Scandinavia Online*, the online editions of its newspapers, *Svenska Dagbladet*, and the international free newspapers (Norland, 2011: 323; Anand and Hood, 2007; Schibsted, 2000). While the Schibsted Board directed the group management to cut costs, this did not end the pursuit of realizing the company's vision from 1995 of becoming digital and Scandinavian. The belief in the digital transformation remained strong, despite the downturn in the financial markets. Therefore, the Schibsted group management was allowed to continue investing in the Internet, such as the newly established online classified company, FINN, *VG Nett*, and *Aftonbladet Nett*, However, the digital investments were now more controlled and with a reduced scope, Birger Magnus recalls: "The areas for cost reductions were primarily *Aftenposten* and *Svenska Dagbladet*, which were also most exposed to the economic cycle. Nor could we continue to invest as much in digital development" (Birger Magnus, interview author, 2024).

FINN – Creating a Disruptive Online Classified Advertising Company

Print newspapers continued to generate major revenues and profits from classified advertisements, but as observed in the second half of the 1990s, this business model faced uncertainty and was to become increasingly under pressure. Terje Seljeseth, IT director and part of the leadership group at the *Aftenposten* newspaper, for which classified advertising made up major parts of its income, was particularly vocal in pushing for more a drastic online classified initiative than the *vis@avisen*'s business model of posting pdfs of printed classified advertisements online. Seljeseth argued for embracing the logic of the Internet fully with a new online classified advertising company (Seljeseth, interview with author, 2024).

Seljeseth was given the task of developing the business plan for the company and was supported by a small team of McKinsey consultant's in this work. The proposal for the new company was presented to the collaborating newspapers, who concluded to realize the plans. In October 1999, the new online classified advertising company, FINN, was established (Seljeseth, interview with author, 2024). However, there were several controversies in relation to the establishment of the new online classified company FINN. First, there were discussions on the size of ownership share between the partners: the national newspaper, *Aftenposten*, and the regional papers, *Bergens Tidende*, *Stavanger Aftenblad*, *Adresseavisen*, and *Fædrelandsvennen*, Didrick Munch, CEO of *Bergens Tidende* and the first chair of the board of FINN recalls (Munch, interview with author, 2024).

However, by late 1999, *Aftenposten* had 62 percent ownership in FINN, and the regional newspapers, *Bergens Tidende*, *Adresseavisen* and *Stavanger Aftenblad* each had a 11.3 percent ownership share, and *Fædrelandsvennen*, the smallest regional newspaper among the partners, had 4 percent share (Schibsted,

40 *Schibsted*

1999). Then, FINN was launched only two days after the dot-com crash (Anand, 2016). Terje Seljeseth, the first CEO of the new FINN company explains:

> We made the first version very quickly, and launched it in March 2000, and then proceeded to establish ourselves in new premises and hire more people and build the technical team and all the things you have to do when you build such a company.
>
> (Seljeseth, interview with author, 2024)

However, what caused the biggest controversy was the fact that Finn was to compete directly for classified advertising with its owners, and the national *Aftenposten* in particular. Terje Seljeseth, points out that it was a very difficult situation: "It was extremely demanding, because it was clear that the company that we built up was certainly a direct threat to the classified ads in the print newspapers, which were, a significant source of income in all five newspapers" (Seljeseth, interview with author, 2023). However, internationally, there were increasingly signs that the print newspapers began losing out in the increased competition from Internet companies offering online classified advertising. Such companies, that is Stepstone and Jobline, emerged also in Norway:

> It was really only FINN in Norway, among the classified players, who were owned by traditional media houses. It is really unique. So, it was an incredibly important time, 2000, 2001, 2002, but it was tough when Schibsted said: 'Ok, if we're going to cannibalize, it's better that we do it ourselves, or else others will come to do it.'
>
> (Munch, interview with author, 2024)

By the end of 2000, FINN had more page visits in the classified market for jobs, real estate, cars, and boats than its main competitors combined (Schibsted, 2000: 19). At the same time, the print newspaper business continued to deliver major profits. In 2000, the print newspapers generated an operating profit of NOK 450 million, an increase of NOK 128 from the year before. The revenues from advertising in the print editions of *Aftenposten, VG, Aftonbladet,* and *Svenska Dagbladet* increased by 11 percent in the same period. Parallel to this, the advertising revenue from the online newspaper editions, including FINN, rose from NOK 69 million in 1999 to NOK 181 million in 2000 (Schibsted, 2000: 7). Then in 2003, Schibsted reported that the company's "venture into new media finally made its breakthrough" (Schibsted, 2003: 5). Didrik Munch, the chair of the board of FINN recalls: "We lost money during the first two years, but then it started going toward zero. In 2002, 2003, that's when it starts to happen, and that's when we gave 'full throttle' on FINN" (Munch, interview with author, 2024). In fact, by 2003, the number of users of FINN increased by

The Emergence of the Digital and International Schibsted 41

50 percent, and the online classified company became the tenth-largest website in Norway in terms of unique users. That year, FINN had a turnover of NOK 135 million and an operating profit of NOK 44 million (Schibsted, 2003: 2). Ole Jacob Sunde, points out that the early success of FINN was key for the company: "A breaking point in the digitalization of classified ads, was the early signs of progress for FINN. The numbers were not impressive, but it gave us the self-confidence to continue investing" (Sunde, interview with author, 2024).

There are a several explanations for why FINN succeeded and so quickly. These relate to the logic of the digital economy, technology innovation, "network effects," and Schibsted's willingness to continue to make digital investments in the wake of the dot-com crisis, and to allow FINN to compete with its newspapers print classified advertising businesses, along with the company's close-knit leadership group driving the digital transformation forward. In fact, Aleksander Rosinski, having had many senior positions within Schibsted's classified operations, including as a Managing Director of FINN Travel, argues that Schibsted's decision to establish FINN was the one decision that set the company apart from other media companies internationally:

> Most of the decisions made by the Schibsted group management were typical, but then they made some decisions that were atypical, and the perhaps biggest of those decisions were FINN. At a time of incredible uncertainty about what the future would entail, a direct competitor to *Aftenposten* was eventually launched, at full speed. FINN was set up as a separate company and was free to compete on price and product with *Aftenposten*. It was a very atypical decision, as companies very rarely make such decisions and operationalize them fully. Companies may say they are open to the idea of cannibalizing oneself and starting independent business units for such activities, but in reality, do not follow through, because they put a lot of restrictions on the new unit or set-up.
>
> (Rosinski, interview with author, 2023)

However, Terje Seljeseth, the originator of FINN, and the first CEO of FINN, points out that the support from the CEO and senior management of Schibsted was decisive in this tense phase (Seljeseth, interview with author, 2024). In 2003, as FINN had begun to generate profit and become the online classified marked leader in Norway, further motivating Schibsted's digital investment and expansion, the senior leadership consisting of CEO Kjell Aamot and the heads of the three company divisions formed a close-knit group: Sverre Munck, EVP for Strategic Projects and Business Development; Birger Magnus, Deputy CEO of Schibsted and EVP for News; and Jan Erik Knarbakk, Executive Vice President of TV/film division. While TV/film operations were phased out and divested throughout the 2000s, Ole Jacob Sunde, Chair

42 *Schibsted*

of the Schibsted Board (2002–2022), points out how these people were key for Schibsted's digital transformation and international expansion:

> Kjell (Aamot) was a strong communicator, I used to call him Schibsted's Foreign Minister. He was also clever in hiring talented managers and Sverre Munck and Birger Magnus were driving forces of the business development. Sverre worked with digitalization and Birger with media. Both were instrumental in developing the digital strategy of Schibsted in the early 2000.
>
> (Sunde, interview with author, 2024)

FINN was Schibsted's first major digital success, and Birger Magnus argues that the reason for its success was twofold:

> The first half of the story is that they restarted in Autumn 1999 and Spring 2000, with a much better organization, with a clearer and more offensive mandate. The other half of the story is that the competition was reduced because the capital markets were not as willing to take risks after the dot. com collapse. All in all, it is very good for Finn. It did not take long before income rose, and we became profitable.
>
> (Magnus, interview with author, 2023)

Sverre Munck argues that the success of FINN was also due to the way the company embraced the logic of Internet in terms of small but many streams of revenue. Furthermore, FINN was not restricted to regional markets, as its owners the regional print newspapers had been. In that sense, FINN became both regional and national, by being a so called "agnostic brand" (Munck, interview with author, 2023).

FINN's success was also due to its ability to achieve "network effects" in only a few years. While well-known today, at the time, very few was consciously aware of how to create such effects, their disruptive consequences, and the major business benefits created by this phenomenon, Rosinski points out:

> The move from print to digital created a situation that often leads to a network being moved from one place to another. This is called a platform change. In a similar way as when users moved from desktop computers to smartphones later, so did the network effects manifest themselves around classified advertising when moving from print to online. It was thought that this was going to happen very, very quickly because when network effects reach their negative inflection point, the marketplace disappears from the old place and re-emerges in the new place.
>
> (Rosinski, interview with author, 2023)

The Emergence of the Digital and International Schibsted   43

To help create such network effects, FINN used the strategy model of "Borrowing, forgetting and inventing" (Anand and Hood, 2007). Rosinski, elaborates:

> That is, borrowing assets from the old, analogue world. FINN and *Aftenposten* and classified advertising, but also *VG Nett* and *VG* print, are examples of this. The new digital company could decide for itself what it wanted to use and borrow from the old company but then forget what it did not want.
> (Rosinski, interview with author, 2023)

This approach became central when developing new digital units or businesses, that was later incorporated into the main company, when deemed strong enough to maintain their distinctiveness in terms of a business model, market position, and corporate culture.

Swedish Expansion in Online Classified Advertising

With confidence from the successful launch and promising development of the online classified company, FINN, in Norway, international expansion of classified advertising business was soon on the agenda. Although FINN had yet to generate profit, in 2000 it had more visits than all its competitors together. That year, Schibsted announced that the FINN concept was to expand internationally (Schibsted, 2000: 19). In 2000, one early move was to enter agreements for cooperation with a number of large media companies in Europe, with the aim to develop the FINN concept (Schibsted, 2001). However, what proved to be the decisive move in the early internationalization was the decision to expand into the Sweden. The acquisition of *Aftonbladet* in 1996, with the number one online newspaper edition in Sweden, provided major opportunities for exploiting the newspaper's Internet traffic, to give marketing support to an online classified site. Schibsted, the company, went ahead with the launch of a version of FINN in Sweden, FINNMER, in 2003, Birger Magnus explains:

> The success of FINN gave us self-confidence, and it gave us credibility and a reasonable degree of trustworthiness within the Schisted group board. Before FINN became a success, we hadn't really succeeded digitally. The online newspapers, especially *Aftonbladet*, were successful, but without any particular profitability. However, the success of FINN in Norway led to the expansion of online classifieds into Sweden. We had the expertise in FINN, and we had the classifieds in *Svenska Dagbladet*, and then we had *Aftonbladet*'s internet traffic.
> (Magnus, interview with author, 2023)

In fact, the technology behind FINN had been turned into the company Finntech, and the idea was to license this technology to media companies internationally

44 *Schibsted*

(Munck, interview with author, 2023). While the idea made sense, in practice it proved much more difficult as "[n]ewspaper companies around the world existed in different media market contexts and they did not think in the same way as Schibsted and FINN had done in Norway" (Rosinski, interview with author, 2023).

Schibsted's Swedish version of FINN, FINNMER, met fierce competition from a small Swedish company, Blocket. Blocket, launched in 1996, was described as "a local buy-and-sell market in Skåne in Southern Sweden," which was "run out of a garage in Fjälkinge by one person" (Schibsted, 2007). Blocket had far less resources, than the Schibsted-owned FINNMER, yet fought off the competition and having achieved "network effect" grew rapidly (Rosinski, interview with author, 2023). Schibsted acknowledged losing out to Blocket, and instead decided to buy the company. Schibsted first bid just under SEK 100 million, at a time when other media companies internationally were careful with online investments in the wake the dot-com crises, but the bid was rejected by the Blocket owners, but succeeded with a SEK 180 million six to nine months later, in 2003 (Munck, interview with author, 2023).

In contrast to the Norwegian newspaper, *Aftenposten*, which relied on the print classified advertising business model, that was cannibalized by the online company, FINN, the print edition of the Schibsted-owned Swedish *Aftonbladet* had not relied on income from classified advertising. Therefore, the digitization of such advertising did not represent any threat to the newspaper's revenues, but instead presented an opportunity. Since 1996, *Aftonbladet* had attempted to launch classified advertising both in print and online, but without success. This changed with the acquisition of Blocket (Barland, 2012: 161). Schibsted's acquisition of Blocket not only represented the successful expansion in Sweden, with the help of the massive Internet traffic from *Aftonbladet*, but the competitive and efficient Blocket concept and technology soon proved to be key for Schibsted's worldwide expansion in online classified as "Blocket clones" was launched internationally.

News Media

How did Schibsted's other key core business area, news media, fare in the wake of the dot-com crash? Just before the crash, in 1999, *Aftonbladet* made a strategic decision that was to be formative for organizational innovation in Schibsted. The Swedish newspaper decided to separate its Internet business from the media house. The aim was to "make both journalists, salespeople and programmers dedicated to the new online medium" (Barland, 2012: 136). This approach was also adopted by the new FINN company launched in 2000. *VG* online was a separate unit to the print newspaper *VG* from 2000 and until 2008, but with a mandate to compete with the *VG* print newspaper. The aim was to develop a distinct corporate culture, different from the culture in the traditional

The Emergence of the Digital and International Schibsted 45

newspaper and make *VG* online journalistically and financially sustainable (Pedersen, interview with author, 2023).

Scandinavia Online, had launched in 1996, and only two years later, it became the most-visited website in Sweden and Norway (Syvertsen et al., 2014: 102). The Internet portal was then stock-listed shortly before the dot-com crash. While *Scandinavia Online* was also launched to compete with the expanding internet portals, American Online never became a competitor in the region as many feared, and some claim that *Scandinavia Online*'s strong position in the portals and search markets was the reason Yahoo! decided to withdraw from the region (Ottosen and Krumsvik, 2012). In the late 1990s, Schibsted believed that *Scandinavia Online* was a key outlet for content and services online, but this proved too optimistic: "While *Scandinavia Online* employed many journalists, it did not have the trust and appeal of the established Schibsted newspaper brands" (Munck, interview with author, 2024). Schibsted's newspapers only contributed with news content and were not integrated in the portal. In the end, the revenues did not justify the major investments in the loss-making portal, and *Scandinavia Online* was sold in 2001. Instead, Schibsted decided to focus on its newspaper brands online. In fact, already by 2002, *VG* and *Aftonbladet*'s online versions were the most read in Norway and Sweden (Schibsted, 2002: 6). Sverre Munck emphasizes that the *Scandinavia Online* initiative showed the senior management of Schibsted group the importance of prioritizing the strong traditional news brands online:

> We had experienced that our strong brands, primarily *Aftenposten*, *VG* and *Aftonbladet*, were the best at producing digital news content. So, they were actually, allowed to continue investing and run losses on the digital parts of their news businesses. It was a kind of reversal of the strategy, where we said: you develop your own brands digitally. However, the strategy for digital classified advertising was not reversed, because we realized we had discovered a business model that worked and that required independence from the individual newspaper. We gave "full throttle" on FINN, while we gave *Aftenposten*, *Aftonbladet*, *VG* and the other regional newspapers the responsibility for running the development of digital news content.
>
> (Munck, interview with author, 2023)

Still, in the wake of the dot-com crisis, in the early 2000s, Norwegian newspapers were experiencing weaker advertising markets, and significant cost reductions were implemented (Schibsted, 2022a). Major cuts were made in *Aftenposten*, and *Svenska Dagbladet* was in financial trouble. However, despite the financial situation, there was a strong belief in the coming of the digital transformation:

> We knew that despite the decline in the capital market in the wake of the burst of the dot.com bubble, the digital transformation was going to happen.

46 *Schibsted*

There was no doubt about that. We were allowed to continue the digital investments by the Schibsted group board, but with a reduced scope and in a more controlled way. The major costs reductions were to a large extent made in the established media businesses.

(Magnus, interview with author, 2024)

VG's online investments and costs were also scrutinized. Several features were removed, and some investments were ended, but the Schibsted newspapers were in general allowed to continue to experiment and develop on the editorial content side (Munck, interview with author, 2024). The separate unit *VG Nett*'s editorial online strategy was to prioritize developments that utilized the characteristics and qualities of the Internet and its distinctive features that would set the online newspaper apart from the traditional print edition. Initiatives focused on sound, live events, and gradually publishing on mobile phones and other handheld devices. In terms of journalistic content, the major sports and political events and more dramatic international news events were key to *VG*'s online growth and development. This happened in particularly two ways: new journalistic approaches emerged from covering such events, and these events drove the increase in visitors and Internet traffic (Barland, 2012: 112–113). Such events, for example the terror attack on the Twin Towers on September 11, 2001, in New York City, had a similar role in *Aftonbladet*'s online development and growth in popularity among readers (Barland, 2012: 136). The online newspaper editions utilized the possibility for minute-by-minute news updates and delivery (Anand, 2016). These online editorial strategies were the key to the phenomenal growth in *VG* and *Aftonbladet*'s online reach and readership. In 2004, *VG* was Norway's largest online newspapers, and *Aftonbladet* by far the most-visited media website in Sweden (Schibsted, 2004). Still, in general, the cost side of the newspapers was not sustainable, as the online revenues did not compensate for the loss of income from print newspapers, that had to make considerable cost reductions, to remain profitable (Munch, interview with author, 2023). The situation for the Swedish, *Svenska Dagbladet*, was particularly serious. Ole Jacob Sunde, the newly appointed Chair of the Board of Schibsted (2002–2022), recalls discussion with Tinius Nagell-Erichsen and Kjell Aamot on whether to close the newspaper or not. However, with Gunnar Stromblad, CEO of the newspaper and Lena Samuelson, Chief Editor, at the helm, they were able to turn around *Svenska Dagbladet* (Sunde, interview with author, 2024).

Schibsted: International and Leading – The New Vision

By 2005, Schibsted had established FINN successful in Norway and had acquired Blocket in Sweden and focused on the newspaper brands online in Norway and Sweden successfully and free newspapers internationally. Its film and TV division had a considerable Norwegian presence through ownership in the national commercial terrestrial television channel, TV2, and the Swedish television

The Emergence of the Digital and International Schibsted   47

channel, TV4, along with ownership in TV and film production and distribution. The company had aimed to become a Nordic television company but did not succeed in taking over TV4 and its owner, the Finish media company Alma Media. The Swedish media company, Bonnier, had, in 2005, stopped Schibsted's plans to take over the Swedish television channel, TV4, and Alma Media changed strategic direction (Sundin, 2013). Birger Magnus elaborates:

> We were invested in the Norwegian TV2 from the start, and we fought to get a position in the television sector in Sweden and Finland. Our ambition was to become Scandinavian also in television, but we couldn't get the building blocks to fit. The failed attempt to buy Alma Media in Finland, which would also have given us TV4 in Sweden, was the beginning of the end for our investments and ownership interests in television.
>
> (Magnus, interview with author, 2023)

However, despite the failure in achieving a Nordic television operation, Schibsted was to launch a vision that extended its ambitious far beyond the region.

In 2005, Schibsted's CEO Kjell Aamot proclaimed the new vision:

> Schibsted has outgrown its former vision – now we're going for Europe! The vision established in 1995 had a Scandinavian perspective – it has served its purpose and is becoming out-of-date. We have come to a point where we must adjust to the current situation and establish our new ambition – to be the most attractive media group in Europe.
>
> (Aamot quoted in Schibsted, 2005: 14)

Birger Magnus, central in the creation of the new vision, explains the development and aims of the new strategy and vision:

> We defined a clear internationalization strategy in 2005 and at the same time we started work to renew our vision and strategy. This work took as a starting point that we had concluded that the vision we had created in 1995, had been realized. We were leading in Scandinavia, and independent of media choice. We didn't have much TV, but we were digital. We wanted a vision that was more inspiring and relevant. The new vision said that we should become a European leader. It said little about products,but a lot about people and the organization. It took as its starting point that the winners are those who manage to achieve a high level of innovation power in the different businesses. How do we work together? How do we develop people? How do we become a leader in innovation?
>
> (Magnus, interview with author, 2023)

The new vision was supported by the increasing influence of young and talented employees emerging from Schibsted's management trainee program, Amandus,

48 Schibsted

launched in 1997, as well as strong financial results. In 2005, Schibsted experienced its best financial result ever, with profits of nearly NOK 1 billion and revenues of NOK 9.8 billion, driven by the company's core businesses strengthening their market positions (Norland, 2011: 326; Schibsted, 2005).

International Expansion of Classified Advertising

Schibsted's online classified operations in Norway, FINN, became profitable in only a few years, and the newly acquired Blocket had a solid market position in its home market, Sweden. Now, further international expansion was on the agenda. While the FINN technology was a success in Norway, it failed in Sweden, due the competitiveness of Blocket's business model concept and innovative technology. In fact, Blocket was to prove just as competitive internationally through the laucnh of "Blocket clones" (Rosinski, interview with author, 2023). Sverre Munck points out that they decided on first launching "Blocket clones" in countries where Schibsted had a media presence, the free newspapers:

> I was already responsible for France and Spain through our free newspapers 20 Minutes in these countries, so I thought: let us try the Blocket business model in Spain and France, and we started in Spain. . . . We launched a "Blocket clone" in Spain in March 2005, called Compraventa, which means buying and selling. It took off like a rocket, despite established players already active in Spain. The technology, the business model and scalability of Blocket was very, very good.
>
> (Munck, interview with author, 2023)

While FINN in Norway connected consumers and retailers within the automobile and real estate sectors, Blocket connected consumers with consumers, Birger Magnus explains:

> Blocket went consumer to consumer (c2c). It was much easier to enter some of the continental markets in this way. The cooperation with intermediaries that FINN did in Norway would take years to develop internationally. So, this was an easier and faster way to expand internationally. In addition, Blocket's technology was of major significance.
>
> (Magnus, interview with author, 2023)

Rolv Erik Ryssdal, having worked in Schibsted since 1991, and the future, second CEO of Schibsted (2009–2018), underlines how the Blocket technology was disruptive by the fact that it attracted and connected consumers, and that retailer then became interested when these online sites generated much traffic (Ryssdal, interview with author, 2024). The acquisition of Blocket, and its central role in international online classified expansion,

The Emergence of the Digital and International Schibsted 49

made it one of the most strategically successful and profitable investments Schibsted has made:

> While one may say that the acquisition of Blocket has perhaps been the most value-creating, if we look at the values that lie in Leboncoin (classified site in France) and part of the other international sites and Blocket itself, but you can also bring it back to *Aftonbladet* and that acquisition. So, often it is like that, and I see that in other contexts as well. When you do a transaction, buy a company, so look carefully at what strategic options that come as a result of that deal. Maybe they are the ones that will create the most value?"
>
> (Ryssdal, interview with author, 2024)

The operationalization of the new vision of Schibsted to become a leading European company gained further momentum when Schibsted acquired the international classified advertising company, Trader Classified Media in 2006 (Schibsted, 2007). As with *Aftonbladet*, this acquisition represented strategic options for the company, yet on a much larger scale and of greater significance. The EUR 553 million acquisition of Trader Classified Media was Schibsted's largest investment to date and included classified operations in Spain, France, Switzerland, Italy, and Latin America:

> Trader was market leader in many countries but had a heavy print component. But I remember in our valuation of Trader we set 5% of the value to print and 95% of the value to the digital potential. Within a year and a half after we had bought the company, we had closed down all the print operations. . . . So, we ended up running Blocket clones in France, Spain and Italy, while we continued with the existing brands in the Trader portfolio in the other countries.
>
> (Munck, interview with author, 2023)

The Trader Classified Media acquisition proved decisive for Schibsted's internationalization, yet also saddled the company with major debt (Schibsted, 2022a). Aleksander Rosinski argues that, while the quality of the assets of the Trader Classified Media company and the price may be debatable, the acquisition had a major impact on Schibsted on a fundamental level:

> The Trader Classified Media transaction changed Schibsted overnight from being a Scandinavian media player to becoming a European classified advertising player. The dynamic it created within Schibsted was absolutely decisive for where we are today. Schibsted did have free newspapers in France and a newspaper in Germany and some assets in Estonia, but the company was strategically and mentally, and in every way, a Norwegian, at most a Scandinavian media company. The managers were Norwegian, and they did not speak English in day-to-day business, but Norwegian. Schibsted's

50 *Schibsted*

businesses were largely in Norway, with a couple of companies and assets outside of the county. The acquisition of Trader Classified Media changed the whole dynamic within the company. It brought international attention, and the company had to change its strategy. The company was forced to rethink its capital allocation, and had to start moving talent, roughly speaking, from Norwegian media throughout Europe. So, this transaction is definitely a milestone for Schibsted.

(Rosinski, interview with author, 2023)

Ole Jacob Sunde agrees and points out that, despite a stretched price, the acquisition of Trader Classified Media was of great significance also for the way Schibsted viewed itself:

It changed our mindset. We realized that we were capable of handling large acquisitions abroad and reinforced our confidence in taking on more risk in reaching global dominance in digital classified sites. It also taught us a lesson in being diligent in our homework, often you don't get what you are presented with.

(Sunde, interview with author, 2024)

The acquisition also signaled to investors, the stock market, and competitors alike that Schibsted was willing and able to make major investments to succeed in its digital and international expansion.

A Leading European Media Company

Schibsted's new vision coincided largely with the general trend in the Nordic media market from around 2005, to concentrating and focusing on core business areas, reducing and ending non-core involvements and investments (Sundin, 2013: 10). In 2005, the failed attempt to take over the Finish TV4 and its main owner, the media company, Alma Media, ended the ambitions of a Nordic television company and a rapid exit from television channel ownership followed. The year after, in 2006, Schibsted sold its stake in the Norwegian TV2 for NOK 1.15 billion, and its stake in TV4 in Sweden was sold for SEK 1.455 billion (Schibsted, 2022a).

Despite increasingly focusing on core areas, the Schibsted group management also embarked new major online ventures: a wholly owned search engine in 2005, as well as its own social media service in 2006; yet both were connected to established Schibsted online newspaper brands, While Schibsted did not see the potential in the online search engine, Kvasir, which they acquired as part of OsloNett in 1995, online search had become increasingly important in terms of advertising a decade later. In 2005, Schibsted pointed out that industry forecasts predicted that 50 percent of online advertising would be generated through search (Schibsted, 2005).

The Emergence of the Digital and International Schibsted   51

Google and Yahoo, with already strong brand names, were looking to expand into classified advertising, news, directories, and mobiles services, with local sales forces, also in the Nordics (Sesam, 2005). Google News had already launched news aggregators in Norway and Sweden by the mid-2000s, and one of Schibsted's responses was its own regionally focused search engine, *Sesam*, in November 2005 (Anand and Hood, 2007: 16). The aim of *Sesam* was to give users a better overview and insight in news online (Schibsted, 2006a: 47). Schibsted believed that Sesam's competitive advantage as a local search engine was local reach and insight in local user habits, local knowledge, and local exclusive content, including news, pictures, directories, and media archives. In addtion, Sesam was "crawling" Norwegian language websites every five minutes, compared to Google who did so every 24 hours. A further key rationale for "local search" was surveys showing a significant growth in the use of Norwegian websites since 1998 (Sesam, 2005; Crampton, 2006).

Schibsted pointed out at the time of its launch that the new *Sesam* would also benefit from the traffic generated from Schibsted's established online brands (Sesam, 2005). Sesam was embedded in *VG Nett*, the online edition of the *VG* newspaper, in 2005 and enabled search both in the online newspaper and on the Internet. A year after its launch, *Sesam* became one of the most popular search services in Norway (Anand and Hood, 2007: 15; Schibsted, 2006a: 39). In the autumn of 2006, *Sesam* was then launched in Sweden, and Schibsted had high hopes for the export of the concept of a "local search engine" internationally (Crampton, 2006). However, Schibsted's foray into search proved far more difficult than expected.

In 2006, Schibsted also launched a social media service, Nettby, or as it was called then, a web community. All content was user-generated and, by the end of 2006, it had 120,000 users in Norway (Schibsted, 2006a: 39). While the Norwegian newspaper, *Dagbladet*, had earlier launched its social media service, Blink, Nettby was run in conjunction with the newspaper *VG*, whose enormous Internet traffic was key to the service's growth. By 2007, Facebook had become the most popular online site in Norway, ahead of both *VG* and *Dagbladet*. Still, the chairman of the Nettby company, Jo Christian Oterhals, did not fear Facebook. Oterhals argued that a key competitive advantage of Nettby was its proximity to its users: "We are close to our users and work actively with the feedback we receive. It is quite a different starting point than the services of Facebook and other similar international online communities" (quoted in Wekre, 2007). As with *Sesam*, Schibsted had international ambitions for Nettby, and particularly in countries such as France and Spain, in which the company owned the free newspaper *20 Minutes*, which could market the local version of Nettby and in which Nettby may be embedded (Huseby Jensen, 2008). However, as with Sesam, Schibsted's move into social media proved far more challenging than many had thought.

52   *Schibsted*

News media and online classified advertising continued to be the core business areas for Schibsted in the new vision of 2005. To succeed in realizing its vision of turning Schibsted into a leading European media company, increased collaboration and joint initiatives between its media houses was seen as key. The major regional newspapers, in which Schibsted by late 2005 owned between 24 and 36 percent, had in the 1990s collaborated in advertising and in launching the pioneering online classified site *vis@avisen*. However, the major collaborative online success was FINN, which was launched in 2000 and jointly owned by *Aftenposten* and regional newspapers: *Bergens Tidende, Stavanger Aftenblad, Adresseavisen*, and *Fædrelandsvennen*. However, in Norway, the company's original home market and its main newspaper market, the idea of a more formal collaboration and consolidation of the subscription newspapers through structural changes was gradually maturing and increasingly discussed (Schibsted, 2022a).

Already in the late 1980s, Birger Magnus then at McKinsey, with colleagues, made a proposal on their own initiative to point out the possibilities for editorial collaboration and sharing between the wholly owned *Aftenposten* and regional newspapers that Schibsted had ownership interests in (Magnus, interview with author, 2023). However, collaboration was mainly limited to advertising sales and distribution, first between three of the regional newspapers, in the 1990s. While McKinsey's proposal argued for collaboration to achieve economies of scale, the situation a decade and a half later was quite different, Magnus points out:

> [T]he forms of economies of scale we saw in 2004 were different from those in 1989. They were based on the digital economy, and required digital platforms and a common way of working. It was far better to coordinate, than to invest in this development separately. The launch of FINN and its success, made people see the need to collaborate.
>
> (Magnus, interview with author, 2024)

The leadership in the newspapers was increasingly preoccupied with this theme, which would eventually lead to a major consolidation of one of Schibsted's wholly owned newspaper and nearly all of the, at the time, co-owned newspapers in the company Media Norge (Munch, interview with author, 2024). Around 2005, at a Schibsted meeting in Antwerp, Belgium, with these newspapers as well as FINN attending, there were discussions about more elaborate collaboration between *Aftenposten, Bergens Tidende, Stavanger Aftenblad, Fædrelandsvennen*, and *Adresseavisen*. In fact, Per Axel Koch, CEO of Adresseavisen; Didrik Munch, CEO of *Bergens Tidene*; and Sverre Munck, Executive Vice President of Schibsted International, "started to discuss if we should merge." Munch reflects, "I was very positive to the idea of growing bigger, together." After the meeting, they agreed that Sverre Munck should take the idea further: "So I think that after that meeting we agreed and said to Sverre: 'You must raise this issue and present the idea with Schibsted centrally. Is there a mood and willingness to do something like this?'" (Munch, interview with author, 2024).

The Schibsted newspapers' discussion on consolidation reflected a more general trend and common strategic direction within the news sector in the face digitization: the establishment of chain ownership (Sjøvaag, 2014: 512–514). While such consolidation may be initiated at corporate group management level, at Schibsted the initiative came mainly from the level of the newspapers. Sondre Gravir, former McKinsey consultant with Schibsted as a key client, having had numerous executive and senior management positions within the company after being hired in 2007 and until 2018, was at first tasked with the Media Norge project. Schibsted was the sole owner of *Aftenposten* and *VG*, and had ownership interests in the regional newspapers, yet did not interfere much with these two media houses and let them run their businesses independently, Gravir argues: "Schibsted had long had a philosophy, which has played a part in Schibsted's success, that the various subsidiaries are part of the same group, but they compete against each other" (Gravir, interview with author, 2024).

Traditionally, the large revenues and profits generated by the print newspapers, with little need for investments in technology, compared to the requirements of digitization, made it possible to run the newspapers independently. This also made the concept of economies of scale an unknown entity for these newspapers, Gravir argues. However, as particularly the revenues from advertising sales declined in the print newspapers, increased collaboration to achieve synergies and cost benefits by investing in digital platforms and technology collectively became necessary (Gravir, interview with author, 2024). It was in this way Schibsted centrally as owner became more involved in the media companies, Gravir believes:

> It was actually what made the (Schibsted) group a more important part and a more important part of the operative side in the media houses. It wasn't that the group forced itself onto them, seen from a Schibsted point of view, as I see it. It was more that you realized that there is a much greater need for cooperation, and you have to somehow find the framework for cooperation.
>
> (Gravir, interview with author, 2024)

In 2006, the merger plans of establishing the media group Media Norge were approved by the boards of directors of the newspapers: *Aftenposten* AS, *Bergens Tidende* AS, *Fædrelandsvennen* AS, *Fædrelandsvennen* Trykkeri AS, *Stavanger Aftenblad* ASA, and Schibsted ASA. The aim was to become a "leading media company" in Norway, while maintaining a strong, independent and regional editorship, and the "main areas of joint efforts within the new group will be new digital products" (Schibsted, 2006b). *Adresseavisen*, in which Schibsted had ownership in, took part in the Media Norge discussions, but decided not not to join. This was partly due to the Norwegian Media Authority's stated concerns over Media Norge's market dominance, that could hinder the establishment of the new news company (Schibsted, 2006c).

While the general trend of consolidation and mergers is "not necessarily-damaging to media plurality," the question of the possible impact on editorial

54 Schibsted

content and journalism is often raised in relation to this development within the news sector. Therefore, several regulatory measures are in place to avoid this (Sjovaag, 2014: 512). In fact, both the Norwegian Media and Competition Authorities, along with competing news media companies, were, for different reasons, critical to the establishment of Media Norge. One of the areas of collaboration was to gather newspaper printing to maximize the use of printing technology and thereby achieve benefits of scale. The Norwegian Competition Authorities were skeptical due to the market position and control Schibsted would gain over the printing of the newspaper *Dagbladet*, the main competitor of the Schibsted-owned newspaper, *VG* (Hjeltnes, 2010: 460–461), but also the dominant position the company would have in classified advertising. All the major, competing Norwegian newspaper companies, Avishuset Dagbladet, Edda Media, A-pressen and Norges Handels og Sjofartstidende, coordinated their protests and arguments in a public hearing organized by the Norwegian Competition Authorities. John Arne Markussen, the then group editor of the Norwegian newspaper *Dagbladet*, and one of the most vocal industry critics, argued:

> In this way, Schibsted gets a totally dominant market position. They will sit on seven of the nine largest newspapers with websites in Norway. In addition, they get control of the printing houses, distribution and product placement in shops. They will gain enormous power with the dealers.
>
> (Markussen cited in DN, 2007, author's translation)

While Schibsted promised the Norwegian Competition Authorities to offer competitive prices for printing, the Norwegian Media Authorities was sterner. There was a widespread worry that Schibsted would become an even more powerful and influential in the Norwegian media sphere. The Norwegian Media Authorities decided against the merger and establishment of Media Norge in 2007, due to ownership regulations, as Schibsted would gain too much market control (Hjeltnes, 2010: 461).

After the Media Norge merger was stopped by the Norwegian Media Authorities, Schibsted complained to the Complaints Board for ownership in the media. In 2008, the Complaints Board decided to accept the merger and establishment of Media Norge, but only if Schibsted reduced its shareholdings in *Adresseavisen* and in the Harstad Tidende Group. However, in 2008, the Harstad Tidende Group became, together with *Adresseavisen*, part of the new major Norwegian news media company, Polaris Media, in which Schibsted had a 43 percent ownership (Schibsted, 2008: 12). One of the conditions for the Appeals Board for Media Ownership accepting the establishment of Media Norge was that Schibsted reduced its ownership share in the recently formed news company, Polaris Media AS (Schibsted, 2008: 21). Historically, Schibsted has faced political restrictions, and the Media Norge merger showed how Schibsted worked to

The Emergence of the Digital and International Schibsted 55

overcome these and adjust to realize its ambitions, not only through negotiations and discussions with the authorities but also by defending the merger publicly in the face of industry critics (Syvertsen et al., 2014: 106). Still, Markussen, the then CEO of the Berner Group and the owner of the newspaper *Dagbladet*, expressed fears for loss of media diversity, arguing that Schibsted had now "gained formidable media power" and "the public debate and conversation will be the loser" (Markussen cited in Spigseth, 2008, author's translation).

The Media Norge company, consisting of *Aftenposten*, *Bergens Tidende*, *Stavanger Aftenblad*, and *Fædrelandsvennen*, could now be formally established. However, the plan was to be hampered by both a major external and an internal crises.

Realizing the Vision and Strategy and the Impact of the Financial Crises

With 9000 employees across 21 countries in 2007, the operationalization of Schibsted's vision of becoming "the most attractive media group in Europe" and its digital transformation and international expansion was going ahead at full speed (Schibsted, 2007; 2008: 9). By 2007, the Swedish Blocket's business model and technology was a key driver of the international expansion of online classifieds, through the launch of "Blocket clones." The company's classified operations now had a presence in 21 countries. That year, Schibsted reported record profits, of which 51 percent came from its online businesses (Schibsted, 2022a). Schibsted was well on its way to establishing Media Norge, the largest news media company in Norway, and by Schibsted considered as a bulwark and proactive strategy in the face of the digital transformation and international competition. While the traditional newspaper and media houses were key for Schibsted's Scandinavian expansion, the free newspapers spearheaded the international media expansion outside the region (Schibsted, 2008: 9). By 2008, Schibsted was Europe's second-largest publisher of free newspapers. As many as 6 million people read daily the free newspapers *20 Minutos* in Spain, *20 Minutes* in France, *15 Min* in Lithuania and Linnaleht in Estonia, as well as the weekly newspaper *Moi Rayon* in Russia. The online versions in Spain and France where particularly popular and were the third and fourth most-visited news websites in these countries respectively (Schibsted, 2008: 17). *Nettby*, Schibsted's social media service in Norway, had more than 800,000 members by the end of 2008 (Schibsted, 2008: 23). The same year, the Nettby concept was exported and launched in Spain (Schibsted, 2008: 17). Year 2008 was also the year that VGNett, the online edition of Schibsted's newspaper *VG* became the most read newspaper in Norway ever, and in Sweden, *Aftonbladet* aimed to become the "foremost disseminator of news" regardless of distribution channel (Schibsted, 2008: 22, 24).

Schibsted's activity did not go unnoticed internationally. In 2007, CEO of Schibsted, Kjell Aamot, was invited by Rupert Murdoch, CEO of News Corp.,

56 *Schibsted*

to address the company's senior management on digital media (Schibsted, 2007). Aamot addressed News Corp. senior executives from across the company within film, TV, and newspapers. Birger Magnus recounts the event:

> The invitation from Murdoch was testimony to our early digital expansion. He (Kjell Aamot) was flown in to a meeting of (News Corp.) managers at a ranch in the US. Here, he was presented as a media CEO who knew how to succeed digitally. For Kjell and us, this was really fun and a feather in our cap.
>
> (Magnus, interview with author, 2024)

However, the situation was to change dramatically. The financial crisis hit the world economy, including the media sector, and hit Schibsted hard. While Schibsted's operating revenues were NOK 13,740 million in 2008, the company's operating profits were down to NOK 822 million from nearly NOK 1,200 million in 2007 (Schibsted, 2008: 5). Schibsted's net debt was record high, reaching over NOK 5 billion, while Schibsted's market cap toward the end of 2008 was NOK 5.7 billion, down from NOK 15.4 billion in 2006 (Schibsted, 2022a). The combination of the financial crises, the print advertisement market dropping from its peak, coupled with large debts, much due to the costly Trader Classified Media acquisition in 2006, had severe consequences for Schibsted. The company embarked on major sales of its television and film holdings and real estate assets and began to close a number of non-core companies and operations and implemented major cost-cutting initiatives (Schibsted, 2022a). While the Sesam search engine had become popular in Norway, the Schibsted Sok company (Schibsted Search), with Sesam as its key asset, lost NOK 126 million in 2006 alone. Then in 2007 it faced major cost reductions, as the number of users was not enough to generate revenues to cover costs. Having lost a total of NOK 500 million since its launch, the ambitious search engine initiative soon became part of the company-wide rounds of business closures, divestments, and cost reductions. In 2008, the company decided to implement dramatic cost-cutting measures that aimed to have an effect of NOK 1 billion in 2009 (Schibsted, 2008a).

In the middle of the financial turmoil, Schibsted worked to finalize the Media Norge merger. One of the last hurdles was to gain full ownership over the regional newspapers, *Bergens Tidende*, *Stavanger Aftenblad*, and *Fædrelandsvennen*, which were to become part of the new company, through acquiring the remining stocks. While the regulatory authorities had approved the merger on certain conditions, despite protests from the industry, the senior management of Schibsted did not agree as to how the acquisition of remaining stocks should be done and even if the whole merger should go ahead. Some argued that it would be too expensive, and the financial crises created market conditions that made these acquisitions not feasible. A dispute erupted particularly between Birger Magnus, Deputy CEO of Schibsted and Executive Vice

The Emergence of the Digital and International Schibsted 57

President of News and central in the development of Media Norge, and Kjell Aamot, the CEO of Schibsted. Magnus recalls:

> In the Autumn of 2008, a situation arose when questions about the transactions and implementation emerged. I had made agreements, on behalf of Schibsted, and promised that we would redeem the ownership positions in the newspapers and do it in a way that was agreed upon, that was clear and predictable.
>
> (Magnus, interview with author, 2024)

However, the financial crises changed the market conditions, and disagreement erupted. Magnus explains:

> Then, suddenly there was a discussion in the Schibsted group management about whether it was right to stand by the promises we had given. I thought we had to stand by them. Others believed that we should instead "squeeze them out" and pick up the shares at a later date. Then we could use force to achieve this. However, I said that if we use force, we will lose legitimacy. If we do, we would not have kept our word, and it would be very difficult to integrate these newspapers in a positive way.
>
> (Magnus, interview with author, 2024)

Didrik Munch, the project leader of Media Norge and then appointed CEO of Media Norge in 2008, recalls: "There was a lot of arguing about whether we should establish Media Norge or not. Kjell Aamot was actually a bit against it. Birger Magnus and he were almost in an open conflict" (Munch, interview with author, 2024). While there was disagreement within the group management, the board decided to approve the proposal for acquiring the remaining shares of the newspapers, and the deals were then followed through. Still, the chair of the Schibsted Board (2002–2022), Ole Jacob Sunde, agrees that the cost of taking control over the newspapers were high:

> In hindsight, one may contemplate whether the price we paid was too steep. However, the transaction gave us a controlling interest in a large part of the print circulation in Norway which has enabled substantial scale effects in the subsequent years. If we fast forward and analyze the next 10-year period, it is quite clear that it was a clever move. But Kjell (Aamot) was right, in the short term, it was expensive, and it might have been a better tactic being patient, waiting to see how it all played out.
>
> (Sunde, interview with author, 2024)

Media Norge was formally established in 2009. The aim of the company was to scale-up joint efforts online, pool resources in technology investments,

58 *Schibsted*

and increase editorial coordination and collaboration. This was to give the four newspapers greater market impact and create economies of scale. The same year, in 2009, Swedish media houses were gathered in Schibsted Sweden. These mergers were to be decisive for the further digitization and competitiveness of Schibsted's Norwegian and Swedish media houses in the years to come.

Conclusion

In the phase, between 2000 and 2009, the digital and international Schibsted developed rapidly. The media system and context, company, and leadership dimensions shaped the corporate strategy-making and operationalization and help explain the dynamic between centralization and decentralization within the company as the digital transformation and international expansion evolved.

In terms of media system, it became clear that the historical positions of the newspapers were beginning to be replicated in the digital market. The Internet portal, *Scandinavia Online*, was sold, and in both Sweden and Norway Schibsted's online newspapers editions were attracting record numbers of readers. The legacy news brands were able to retain their strong positions also in the digital domain.

As for the leadership dimensions, following the crisis in 1999, the relationship between Kjell Aamot and Tinius Nagell-Erichsen became even closer, with some describing it as "symbiotic." Schibsted's senior executives and management, fronted by Sverre Munck and Birger Magnus, were given a mandate to continue the digital and international expansion, but were instructed to be more cautious and disciplined in their digital investments. Still, this phase is marked also by continued experimentation and risk-taking, in line with Aamot's management style, including a costly foray into the development of a search engine, Sesam. In terms of leadership, in this phase, Ole Jacob Sunde, long-time financial advisor to Tinius Nagell-Erichsen, became central in the development of Schibsted. Sunde became Chair of the Schibsted board in 2002. Sunde had also been board member of the Tinius Trust, since its inception in 1996 and was promoted to the Chair of the Trust's board in 2007, when Nagell-Erichsen passed away. Sunde took a hands-on approach to the company's decision-making and operations, not least in relation to the financial and transactional side and was in close contact with Aamot, Munck, and Magnus throughout the first decade of the 2000s. The involvement of Sunde represented a further professionalization of the Tinius Trust's board and leadership. The recruitment of relevant competence, aligning the remit of a trust or foundation as owner and the company's corporate strategies for growth and expansion, has been seen as key for creating a competitive advantage for such Nordic news media companies (Achtenhagen et al., 2018: 147).

In terms of company dimensions, the combination of Schibsted's willingness to continue to invest in the digital in the wake of the dot-com crisis and many of its competitors avoiding or reducing their digital investments gave

The Emergence of the Digital and International Schibsted 59

Schibsted speed and advantage in the digital market. This points to Doyle's (2013: 28) argument that recessions are linked to "creative destruction" as resources are often reallocated and companies that either are slow or even resist change are weeded out, while the ones that innovate and are proactive benefit, gain competitive advantages, and take new market positions.

While the company board instructed the leadership to be more cautious, the digitization of Schibsted continued, and so did the experimentation and risk-taking. As Google began to internationalize, Schibsted launched its own Sesam search engine, aiming for regional dominance, and as Facebook expanded overseas, Schibsted and its newspaper, *VG*, launched its own social media service, Nettby. While the Schibsted newspapers attracted readers, the challenge was how to create sustainable business models that enabled the monetization of the increasing online readership and Internet traffic. The print newspapers were facing increased competition for classified advertising from online businesses. A decisive strategic move was the online classified site, FINN, launched on the initiative of – and owned by the Schibsted newspapers. While FINN cannibalized the newspapers' classified operations, it was to succeed in transferring this business area into the online domain. With FINN, Schibsted could exploit the "winner-takes-all" network effect, and the company became profitable in 2003. The acquisition of the Swedish classified site, Blocket, in 2003 marked the establishment of both major news media and classified advertising presence in Norway and Sweden. In 2005, the new vision of Schibsted becoming the most attractive European media company also pointed to an emphasis on organizational development. The Schibsted trainee program, Amandus, was becoming increasingly central in fostering new managers with experience from across the company. This contributed to developing a corporate culture aiming to embrace a more company-wide and international perspective, particualrly at the management level.

The success of FINN and Blocket in the home markets, Sweden and Norway, spurred international expansion. Blocket's disruptive technology and business model enabled the intense international roll-out of online classified sites, increasing the financial potential and value of Schibsted. This points to common, general reasons for international expansion: limited potential for growth in the home market, growth in share value, and the spreading of risk (Hermanni, 2023: 6). While Schibsted's international expansion clearly contributed to realizing the 2005 strategy and vision of becoming a leading European media company, the strategy accentuated one of the challenges for Schibsted's company structure. Schibsted's investments in its international classified intensified, but funding for media was becoming more limited as investors and the stock market considered it a far less attractive investment. This marked the emergence of a certain unease in terms of the "Principal-Agent Problem" (Artero and Manfredi, 2016: 53) between the senior management and investors and the largest owner, the Tinius Trust, dedicated to news media through its Articles of Association.

Media Norge was formally established in 2009 to develop the competitiveness of newspapers online, through cost efficiency, collaboration, and pooling

60 *Schibsted*

resources for major technology investments. Yet the formation of the major new Norwegian newspaper company, in the middle of the financial crisis, led to considerable disagreement within the leadership group. The financial crisis prompted the final divestment and exit from TV and film, sale of real estate, and major cost-cutting programs. The failed search engine, Sesam, exemplifies the risks associated with innovations, in terms of the speed of development and launch in the market, and how innovations are received in the market (Hermanni, 2023: 18). Google represented too fierce a competition, leading to the closure of Schibsted's regionally focused search engine. As with the dot-com crisis, the financial crises spurred the reallocation of resources, strategic refocus, as well as innovation (Doyle, 2013). Several innovations underpin key developments throughout the first decade of the 2000s within Schibsted. The online newspaper edition's focus on exploiting the characteristics of the Internet gathered speed around the dot-com crash. The launch of FINN in 2000, along with *VG*'s online unit, applied a strategy of lending and appropriating assets and resources from the main legacy companies to establish themselves (Anand and Hood, 2007). The formation of separate business units, to develop new digital companies or units, represented a key organizational and business innovation. In the same year as FINN was launched, in 2000, *VG Nett*, the online edition, was established outside the print newspaper *VG* to foster a new digital corporate culture, innovation in online journalism separate from print journalism, and a sustainable online business, while at the same time competing with the legacy newspaper. This exemplifies organizational or structural ambidexterity, as new units are developed outside the main company and then later integrated (Harland, 2018: 3). It also exemplifies the significant cultural changes in news organizations in the face of the digital in this phase (Picard, 2010: 377). In Sweden, the newspaper, *Aftonbladet*, pioneered the utilization of its enormous Internet traffic to promote and build new online companies and services throughout this phase and eventually leading to a new business area, growth, and venture, alongside classified advertising and news media. The relation between Schibsted and McKinsey continued in this phase. The management consultancy was involved in key strategic initiatives including in developing FINN and in the shift from broadsheet to tabloid format of newspapers. As in the second half of the 1990s, in some instances McKinsey consultants with a close working relationship with Schibsted were hired into key positions within the company.

4 Streamlining, New Digital Business Models, and Global Ambitions
2009–2014

The financial crisis hit Schibsted hard and had wide-reaching consequences. The company had to decide rapidly how to move forward. There were several major issues at stake that gave insight into the dynamic between centralization and decentralization and autonomy within Schibsted. The company faced immense pressures from banks and investors who lost confidence in the company, as the value of the Schibsted stock decrease dramatically. While a business model for online classified advertising had been successfully exported internationally, it became more and more clear that its media businesses in the home markets Norway and Sweden had yet to find a sustainable digital business model. Still, by, 2009 as much as 59 percent of the operating profits of Schibsted came from online activities. However, international online classified advertising was increasingly seen as the company's major growth business, in contrast to the media businesses, by the senior management, shareholders, investors, and the stock market. This had consequences not only for the allocation of resources but also for the organization of Schibsted and digital innovation. Consolidation of the news businesses in the home markets, coupled with major investment requirements in the international roll-out of classified advertising sites, and the streamlining of the company, were key corporate strategies in this period. Within news media, in particular, the need to innovate became more and more acute, as the search for new digital business models intensified, but also in terms of organizational innovation, leadership and corporate culture seen as key to succeed in the digital transformation. In fact, already early on in this period, Schibsted's corporate decisions on how to prioritize, organize, and innovate at a challenging time set out the shape and form the company for many years to come.

Crisis, Cost-Cutting, and Consolidation

In the middle of the financial crises, yet another major development happend. The CEO of Schibsted, Kjell Aamot, announced his resignation, leaving the company no later than March 2010 (Schibsted, 2008: 12). Having been in charge of

DOI: 10.4324/9781003439431-4

62 *Schibsted*

the modernization, digitization, and internationalization of the company for over 20 years, Aamot was in a far less protected position after Tinius Nagell-Erichsen, the largest owner in Schibsted, whom he had a strong relationship with, passed away in 2007, and the conflict emerging in 2008 between Aamot and Birger Mangus over Media Norge had created a challenging situation within the group leadership. Following the decision to appoint Rolv Erik Ryssdal as the new CEO, Birger Magnus, Deputy CEO of Schibsted and Executive Vice President of News since 1996, emphasized that it was not an alternative to remain at Schibsted:

> Then came the financial crisis, and I left a bit after it. I was not chosen as the new CEO of Schibsted. It was Rolv Erik (Ryssdal) who was appointed. I had been his mentor and boss, and he had not been in the group management previously. I was number two (in Schibsted), and it wouldn't work for him with me at the table. I took up quite a lot of space and would have had to put a lot of restraint on myself if I continued.
>
> (Magnus, interview with author, 2024)

In 2009, it was announced that Birger Magnus would leave Schibsted after 13 years.

The company faced deepening challenges from the financial crisis. That year, in 2009, Schibsted's advertising revenues fell by 18 percent (Schibsted, 2009b). Ryssdal recalls the beginning of his tenure as the new CEO:

> If you look at the share price, it's like going back the dot.com crash, because this was under and after the financial crisis, and a company that generates its income mainly from advertising revenue is of course very hard hit.
>
> (Ryssdal, interview with author, 2024)

The banks were worried about the size of the company's debt, but Ole Jacob Sunde argued, at the time, that there was nothing financially wrong with the company:

> The refinancing was a difficult period. Schibsted was able to service its loan portfolio. However, we were in breach with our convents and the banks lost their heads, in my view. Schibsted was suffering a steep fall in advertising due to the financial crisis, but we were still a solid company and had a positive cash flow. The atmosphere was depressed, the fear of the banking system going bust was real. The banks forced us to emit shares despite our solidity. The subscription price was rock bottom and value dilutive. It was a period where you had to take a deep breath and look at what was happening with perspective. Was there anything fundamentally wrong with our strategy or operations? No, not really, just that the markets had plummeted, it would come back.
>
> (Sunde, interview with author, 2024)

Streamlining, New Digital Business Models, and Global Ambitions 63

Despite the positive revenue stream, the company needed major financing to reassure the banks, due to the uncertainty in the markets. Shortly before CEO Kjell Aamot left the company, he announced a controversial, yet oversubscribed rights issue (Schibsted, 2009b). In 2009, June 1, when Rolv Erik Ryssdal took over as the new CEO of Schibsted, he was immediately tasked with the capital raising, the implementation of the already-approved major cost reduction, and profitability program (Schibsted, 2022a). Still, Ryssdal argues that it was in fact a very good time to take over as the company was sound in his view (Ryssdal, interview with author, 2024).

The company's divestment activity intensified throughout 2009, selling off several companies that were considered outside its core business activities (Schibsted, 2009b: 29). The most significant media divestment, which also changed the company, was the sale of the remaining film and television business assets, previously part of one of the company's three main divisions. While ownership in the Norwegian TV2 and Swedish TV4 had been divested already in 2006, the sale of the other film and television businesses followed in 2009 as Metronome Film & Television was sold for SEK 719 million (Schibsted, 2009a). The same year, in 2009, Schibsted decided to close its online search engine, Sesam, which had lost around NOK 500 million. The year after, Nettby, Schibsted's social media service also closed. Google and Facebook had rapidly achieved superior market positions, proving impossible for Schibsted's regional search engine and social media service to compete with.

In 2009, Rolv Erik Ryssdal, the newly appointed CEO of Schibsted, oversaw a controversial capital raising of a total of NOK 1.3 billion through the issuing of new shares. The proceeds were used to pay down company debt. However, the market cap of the company had continued to decrease dramatically from NOK 5.7 billion in late 2008, to below NOK 3 billion ahead of this capital raise (Schibsted, 2022a). Raoul Grünthal, soon to be appointed the first CEO of Schibsted Sverige, argues that the Tinius Trust's decision to take part in the capital raise, despite the very low share value and the market's lack of confidence in the company was a daring, but decisive move:

> It was an important detail in Schibsted's history. If the Trust had not been able and willing to do a new issue then we would have had to just save, save and just survive for a period. Then, we would never have gained the speed we gained back in 2011, 2012, but we would have had perhaps another 2–3 years in just survival mode. It was a very important decision.
>
> (Grünthal, interview with author, 2024)

A further strategic financial measure was the reinforcement of cost reduction and profitability programs, with the aim to have an effect of NOK 1.6 billion in 2011 (Schibsted, 2022a).

These major measures aimed to steer the company through the financial challenges and enable the continuing digital transformation and international

64 *Schibsted*

expansion. The new CEO of Schibsted, Rolv Erik Ryssdal, argues that the "financial crisis triggered the situation, but one had also had a very expansive line within the company, where all flowers were allowed to bloom," but this was soon to change:

> There was an understanding of the crisis within the company. So, what I defined, with the help of that board and the new management group, was: 'There are two things we are good at, the media houses we own and run, and that is our legacy, and we will always be doing that, and then there is classified advertising, for which there is still a big opportunity internationally.' I had defined that the year before, in 2008 when I became CEO of Schibsted Classified Media (the company's international online classified operations in 15 countries). So, there was a gathering around this. Those are the two things that we shall be good at. That was the strategy we followed in the years to come, and which I believe was very successful.
>
> (Ryssdal, interview with author, 2024)

By 2009, Schibsted consisted of 7,500 employees in 26 countries, with three divisions: Norway, Sweden, and International, which was organized around the two "strategic axes" and focus areas: the media houses and the expansion of online classified services internationally. The vision of the company stated: "Schibsted will be the most attractive media group in Europe, through people who dare, who challenge and who create" (Schibsted, 2009b: 5) and was to be achieved through the two core business areas. That year, as much as 59 percent of the operating revenues came from online activities (Schibsted, 2009b). The year before, in 2008, the international classified advertising operations had been organized as a separate company, Schibsted Classified Media (SCM). While the financial crisis led to major economic weakening and reduced investments among media companies internationally, Schibsted continued to expand its international classified operations (Schibsted, 2022b). By 2009, SCM had online classified operations in 19 countries, and the majority of the sites were "Blocket clones" (Schibsted, 2009b). That year, the Norwegian newspapers and media houses, *Aftenposten*, *Fædrelandsvennen*, *Stavanger Aftenblad*, and *Bergens Tidende*, had become organized in the Media Norge company (Schibsted, 2022a), and Schibsted Sverige was established and was organized in a similar way, gathering the companies *Aftonbladet* and the *Svenska Dagbladet* (Schibsted, 2009b: 4). In fact, the third CEO of Schibsted, Kristin Skogen Lund (2018–2024), argues that by that time, much of the structure of the future Schibsted was in place:

> It is important to emphasize that it was the executive directors Sverre Munck and Birger Magnus who were the brains behind what happened. They were there until around 2010, and then the foundation was laid, which has since been continued with the culture and mindset that was in place then. We

Streamlining, New Digital Business Models, and Global Ambitions   65

could have ended up as a really old-fashioned media company, if it wasn't for this early foresight.

(Skogen Lund, interview with author, 2023)

However, while the foundation was in place, Schibsted's future success depended on a number of different factors, decisions and developments, within the two key business areas: news and online classified advertising.

News Media

Five key areas are here highlighted as particularly important when explaining the digital transformation of news media in this challenging, but decisive period: collaboration and coordination, a new generation of newspaper editors and directors, digital innovation through autonomous units, the establishment of Schibsted Norge, and the successful introduction of digital news subscriptions. All five areas exemplify the dynamic between centralization and decentralization, shaping Schibsted's strategic decision-making.

Collaboration and Coordination

It was demanding for the newspapers to handle the combination of the decline in print advertising revenue, lack of an online advertising business model, and major cost-cuttings, and at the same time focus on coordination and collaboration between the newspapers within the new Media Norge company (est. 2009) and later in Schibsted Norge (est. 2012). Trine Eilertsen, Chief Editor of *Bergens Tidende* (2008–2012), before moving to *Aftenposten* in 2014, and appointed Chief Editor from 2020, points out how, in the wake of the financial crisis, with changes in reading patterns, and lack of in-house technology competence meant that collaboration and freeing up of resources were more important than ever (Eilertsen, interview with author, 2023). In the autumn of 2012, as part of the Schibsted newspapers' major cost-cutting and personal reductions, 300 staff was sacked, while the editorial changes included that: "central production features were reduced, and syndication was introduced in the sport and lifestyle sections" (Sjøvaag, 2014: 512). While the leaders of the Schibsted newspapers acknowledged the situation and the need to act, Trine Eilertsen points out that it "was challenging to combine all those messages," both in *Aftenposten* and in Bergens Tidende:

It was a very traumatic time for the organization. We didn't lose money. We didn't have red numbers, so it was strategic cost-cutting and downsizing and it was incredibly difficult to make a proper argument for it in a way that the employees were on board with. So, to this day people talk about that 2012 round as very painful and very difficult. It was then the slightly

66 *Schibsted*

hateful tone towards Schibsted as owner began to develop in the editorial offices. We had a two-leader model in all the houses at that time, a director and an editor. However, this initiative did come from us, the editors, and it was very difficult to get heard by our employees, because they thought that it was Schibsted who somehow imposed a demand for savings or a demand for cuts, but it came from us. Schibsted said if you think it is right thing to do for the future of these media houses, then you must manage it, so it is important for me to emphasize that it was initiated by us.

(Eilertsen, interview with author, 2024)

Several processes ran in parallel, but they were not necessarily connected causally. The newspapers were in difficulty due to the financial crisis, while at the same time they were drawn closer together. This created a certain tension, yet was decisive for the survival of the newspapers, Trine Eilertsen argues:

I have spent many hours at general meetings arguing that if it was not for Schibsted who was willing to invest in technology and platforms, and that we were able to use this leeway they had because FINN was doing so insanely well, then I am not sure that we would have survived.

(Eilertsen, interview with author, 2023)

The CEO of Schibsted, during this period, Rolv Erik Ryssdal, argues that, in hindsight, the restructuring and cost-cutting was painful but necessary to prepare the newspapers for the future:

If you look at it in today's light, the very fact that the necessary changes were made has meant that the media houses have had a much better life and were better prepared for the future, than those who did not do it. Of course, these processes were also painful, but we did say all the time that we support new ventures and the development of the companies.

(Ryssdal, interview with author, 2024)

However, the restructuring and implementation of changes was highly dependent on proactive and pragmatic editors and directors of the newspapers, as pointed out in the next section.

A New Generation of Newspaper Editors and Directors

While the rationale for establishing Media Norge (est. 2009) was to strengthen the newspapers digital transformation and market position, by pooling and coordinating resources to enable the major technologic investments, and produce and share content across companies, the success of the merger depended much on the leaders of the newspapers. A new generation of editors and directors emerged in the Schibsted-owned newspapers during this period. The fact that many of them

Streamlining, New Digital Business Models, and Global Ambitions 67

agreed and accepted the need to collaborate and coordinate much closer across newspapers was key. Didrik Munch, CEO of Media Norge, and later Schibsted Norge (est. 2012), points out "To fight against all the editors would be absolutely impossible. So, I spent an incredible amount of time on this, and the editors were quite a large part of the management team that I had" (Munch, interview with author, 2024). However, there was also disagreement when operationalizing Media Norge. Birger Magnus, Deputy CEO of Schibsted and Executive Vice President of News , points out, particularly from the largest newspaper:

> There was opposition from *Aftenposten*, because the newspaper went from having a very clear number one position in Schibsted to being one of several newspapers. It was not the case that the new company (Media Norge) was a subsidiary of *Aftenposten*. Instead, *Aftenposten* became more equal to the others. So, there was a lot of resistance in Aftenposten, and I remember spending time with Kristin Skogen Lund (CEO) and Hans Erik Matre (Chief Editor). They were very loyal, but they didn't really like it. Getting them to be enthusiastic was a bit of a challenge.
>
> (Magnus, interview with author, 2024)

Didrik Munch, points out that an important factor was that he was able to hire and recruit several of the editors and senior management of the newspapers that were part of Media Norge:

> There is also something about the people you hire yourself. You can set the terms a bit. Of course, they have their editorial integrity. It was never questioned, but they had a bit more ownership to the concept and our project (Media Norge).
>
> (Munch, interview with author, 2024)

The digital transformation gathered pace, supported by this new generation, according to one of them, Gard Steiro, Chief Editor of *Bergens Tidende* (2012–2015) and Chief Editor and CEO of *VG*, since 2017:

> You get new managers in during this period. You bring in new editors, younger editors. In *Bergens Tidende*, Trine Eilertsen begins as Chief Editor, then I, and then Øyulf Hjertnes. You bring forth a new generation among the leadership. On the director side, Siv Juvik Tveitnes, Sondre Gravir, and Andreas Thorsheim. There is a generational change in the leadership of the newspapers, that is quite clear on the digital direction.
>
> (Steiro, interview with author, 2023)

This brings us to the next important area in relation to the digital transformation of Schibsted's news media: the relation between digital innovation and organizational structure.

68 *Schibsted*

The Importance of Structural Autonomy in Digital Innovation

The Norwegian online classified company, FINN, is perhaps the most successful example of Schibsted's approach to building a new digital company by first establishing an autonomous company structure. The FINN company was launched in early 2000 in the Norwegian media market to attract online classified advertising and competed directly, particularly with *Aftenposten*'s print classifieds:

> I think one of the most important things, was the understanding very, very early on, that the internet would entail a lasting change, and that you could not defend yourself against it, but that you had to embrace it. There was a realization that you had to do it on the terms of the new medium.
>
> (Skogen Lund, interview with author, 2024)

While variations of this approach have been utilized throughout Schibsted's digital transformation (i.e. Anand and Hood, 2007; Anand, 2016), Gard Steiro argues, in general, such independent units or companies can move faster on their own and can then be integrated into the main company later, when deemed appropriate:

> Those who have dared to cannibalize, and understood changing business models, and made that shift, they have succeeded faster and better than those who have not. It has been important to have sufficient power to build up autonomous units in a critical phase. If not, these environments become too much influenced by legacy media culturally. As independent units, they can also move faster than they can if they are an integral part of legacy media. So, I would say that, if you see the digital development in phases, then you have a phase characterized by a certain playfulness from when you start moving into the digital domain and until about 2008/2009.
>
> (Steiro, interview with author, 2023)

In the late 2000s, as the Internet became more and more important and the digital transformation gathered pace, Schibsted prioritized resources to implement this approach across the company. Gard Steiro explains:

> You managed to create autonomous units. And I think it is an important factor also that Schibsted had the finances to do this. They had such good income from the print newspapers, that they managed to finance the unprofitable digital developments for quite a few years.
>
> (Steiro, interview with author, 2023)

Within news media, a key example of this strategy is the newspaper *VG*'s organizational approach to digital innovation. The newspaper *VG*'s online edition was a separate unit already from 2000 and, until 2011, organized outside the legacy print newspaper *VG*'s organization. The aim was to develop a distinct corporate culture, different from the culture of the traditional print newspaper

Streamlining, New Digital Business Models, and Global Ambitions 69

and make *VG* online journalistically distinct and financially sustainable, Torry Pedersen explains. Pedersen who was central in *VG*'s digital transformation, as editor of *VG Nett* from 2000 to 2008, and later Chief Editor and CEO of *VG*, and holding leading positions in Schibsted Norway, explains: "In 2010, we established *VG Mobil* as a separate company. It only lasted until 2013, because mobile grew so dramatically fast, and then we established the web TV unit, *VGTV*, as a separate company again in 2014" (Pedersen, interview with author, 2023). The new companies had to be independent but, importantly, innovative in terms of both its journalism and market development:

> The newly established companies or units must be independent. They must be innovative in storytelling techniques and develop the market. Move boundaries. Do things that others have not done. Those who have capital receive capital grants from the mothership. This way of organizing creates innovation. You bootstrap them a bit, because they must not get too many resources either. It's about getting to dry land, and preferably as quickly as possible. I believe this has been a key factor for *VG*'s digital success.
>
> (Pedersen, interview with author, 2023)

This approach is often referred to as structural or organizational ambidexterity. As companies need to innovate to remain relevant, competitive and profitable, "the more stable revenues earned from the traditional business need to be maintained, forcing firms to manage two divergent processes to ensure their future success" (Harland, 2018: 3). One way of doing this is through structural ambidexterity, or structural separation, which "entails not only separate structural units for exploration and exploitation but also different competencies, systems, incentives, processes, and culture – each internally aligned" (O'Reilly and Tushman, 2008: 192, quoted in Harland 2018: 6). Pedersen points out "[t]he concept of 'structural ambidexterity,' has been absolutely essential," for *VG* (Pedersen, interview with author, 2024).

The Establishment of Schibsted Norway

While Schibsted Sweden was established already in 2009, a similar national organization, Schibsted Norge, was established in 2012. The latter gathered the news media company Media Norge, and the newspaper *VG*, and the national online classified company, FINN. The initiative Schibsted Vekst (Growth), the emerging digital venture unit, was also included. The aim was to "strengthen Schibsted's digital transformation process and give the company a more innovation power," according to Torry Pedersen, the then Chief Editor of *VG*, now part of the new company Schibsted Norge (Pedersen quoted in Hauger, 2012a). One of the key things that happened in the wake of the establishment of Schibsted Norge was that the CEO of the new company, Didrik Munch, also became the chair of the board of all the five newspapers of the company. This was done to push the digital integration of the newspapers further: "I became chairman of

70 *Schibsted*

all the newspapers, so then we tightened up a bit so that we got increased pressure on the digitization process, and we started to coordinate a lot more of the joint services" (Munch, interview with author, 2024). The fact that *VG* became part of Schibsted Norge had a considerable impact on the drive to digitize the newspaper further. "One of the things that springs from that is the *VGTV* venture," Gard Steiro, Chief Editor and CEO of *VG*, points out, however, at the time: "one is not able to involve Schibsted's smaller regional newspapers to the same extent, as it becomes a game of scale, where *VG* is so large and has become such an important traffic engine" (Steiro, interview with author, 2023). Schibsted and *VG* made major investments on developing and finding a business model for *VGTV*. McKinsey, involved in the corporate development of Schibsted since the late 1980s, was also involved:

> McKinsey has been involved a lot. We used McKinsey in Media Norge and Schibsted Norway, and especially when we were developing *VGTV* and to find a business model for *VGTV*. Around 2012, we created Schibsted Norge, and then we chose to give "full throttle" on *VGTV*. We lost NOK 60–70 million a year, which was very tough. But we persevered and today it is a big, absolutely decisive thing for the whole of Schibsted, at least for the media business side.
>
> (Munch, interview with author, 2024)

The breakthrough in the Swedish *Aftonbladet*'s successful distribution of video online also took place around 2010. Importantly, the rollout of broadband, particularly mobile broadband in Norway and Sweden, was also key to creating the conditions for Schibsted's two largest newspaper's expansion into video and web TV, at the time (Barland, 2012: 142).

The Introduction of the Online Subscription Business Model

The establishment of Schibsted Norge in 2012 led to further integration and coordination, and this proved decisive for developing an online business model solution for its newspapers. While the Nordic online advertising market was dominated by display advertising, a market that grew in the first decade of the 2000s, there was a "temporary slowdown" in the wake of the financial crises and for some years after (Lindberg, 2023: 28). In the early and mid-2010s, newspapers hoped that digital advertisement sales would become the key income, as "[t]he idea was to attract advertisers, through extensive traffic, whose investments would pay for the journalism" (Lindberg, 2023: 88). However, as with other newspaper companies, it had become gradually clear also for Schibsted that the "page view economy" would not generate enough profit, Gard Steiro, Chief Editor and CEO of *VG*, argues (Steiro, interview with author, 2023).

The Norwegian newspaper, *Dagbladet*, was first in the country to establish a digital solution for authentication in 2000. However, *Dagbladet* was not

Streamlining, New Digital Business Models, and Global Ambitions 71

able to include other media companies in this solution. Schibsted established Schibsted Payment in 2011, and their SPID system was used for both login and transactions for Schibsted's online outlets (Krumsvik, 2014: 139). The urgency of creating a financially viable digital business model was further spurred in the early 2010s by the major decline in print advertising, while income from the online businesses did not compensate (Schibsted, 2022a).

Gard Steiro, highlights three key developments in relation to user payment for content and services that took place in this period. The first was Vektklubben (The Weight club) in *VG* in 2005, the launch of an iPad edition of *VG* in 2010, and the third, and most important, the introduction of online subscriptions in the Schibsted newspapers from 2012 onward. Already in 2003, the Swedish newspaper *Aftonbladet* introduced user payment for Viktklubben, a service for users who wanted to lose weight (Barland, 2012: 137). The concept was copied by the Norwegian newspaper *VG* in 2005:

> The first large user payment product that I know of is Viktklubben, which was developed in *Aftonbladet*, and then copied by *VG*. It is, in a way, the first concept where you actually pay for something. I perceive *Aftonbladet* as incredibly innovative. Very active. Lots of spin-offs. It is a digital media house with a lot going on around it. They develop many new digital services, and *VG* takes over part of these services. They copy them and do them in Norway.
>
> (Steiro, interview with author, 2023)

The second initiative for user payment emerged in 2010, as *VG+* was launched. This was the first iPad newspaper version in Norway, and a year after it was named the best iPad newspaper in the world by the World Association of Newspapers (Fossbakken, 2011). At first, *VG+* was free of charge, yet a year after, in 2011, a paywall was introduced, paying via iTunes (Barland, 2015: 126).

The third development in terms of user payment was to become the most significant for the Schibsted's newspapers. The local newspaper *Hallingdølen* is widely credited as creating the first paywall in 2011 in Norway, making most of the online content only available to print subscribers. However, the year after, Schibsted Norge's smallest regional newspapers, *Fædrelandsvennen*, had developed and launched a new user payment subscription model. The formation of Media Norge (est. 2009) and Schibsted Norge (est. 2012), and the fact that Didrik Munch was both the CEO of the company and chair of the board of all the five newspapers enabled a far stronger collaboration between the newspapers. A key corporate initiative was to find a digital business model for the newspapers, other than advertisements, and this project was called "X-files":

> We called the project "The X-files." No one believes it until they see it. Because, at the time there was a lot of doubt. Do we believe in this? How willing were people to pay? There were some who had tested it a little before. These very small newspapers, like *Hallingdølen* (a local Norwegian

72 *Schibsted*

newspaper), but when we did it with *Fædrelandsvennen*, it was relatively large by Norwegian standards. So, then we shut down pretty much everything in *Fædrelandsvennen*. Then, I was chairman of the board at the newspaper, and then I remember we had a lot of discussions about this.

(Munch, interview with author, 2024)

Schibsted's SPID technology formed the basis for this new user payment solution at *Fædrelandsvennen* (Hauger, 2012b). The newspaper had experienced a loss of 11,000 print subscriptions since 1995, but this negative trend ended with the conversion of existing subscribers to digital subscriptions in 2012 (Fossbakken, 2012). In 2012, *VG+* was expanded from being only offered as iPad and iPhone versions to the newspaper *VG*'s main platform for user paid content, including the web version (Barland, 2015: 126). Digital subscriptions and paid content were now seen as the solution newspapers had sought for years. The year 2013 was even by some dubbed "the year of the paywall" not only in Norway but also internationally as digital subscription solutions were implemented widely (Sjovaag, 2015: 304). In January 2013, *VG+* had around 11,000 subscribers, which had increased to 33,000 a year after (Barland, 2015: 126). In 2013, *Aftenposten* started experimenting, and then in 2015 launched a full user payment service, despite uncertainty, yet experienced success rapidly. Trine Eilertsen, Chief Editor of *Aftenposten*, recalls:

We had growth in pure digital subscriptions from around 20,000 to70–80,000 in 2–3 years. No one in the world had faster growth in digital subscriptions, at that time. It went very well and there was money in it, and we got paid. We were very happy then and got people internally to join and to be concerned with digital target figures.

(Eilertsen, interview with author, 2023)

That year, in 2015, around two-thirds of Norwegian and Swedish newspapers had implemented paywalls (Sjovaag, 2019).

In the second half of the 2010s, and early 2020s, most paid newspapers throughout the Nordic region had introduced forms of digital payment solutions for its media content and other services (Lindberg, 2023: 88). The successful development of a user payment model for the Schibsted newspapers was also due to the size of Schibsted group and the ability to innovate in one part of the company and then implement the new digital business model throughout the company. Steiro argues:

This is also an example of how the Schibsted group manages to initiate a fairly large project in one of the media houses, and where they draw experience from it, and can then do the same in the other media houses. One dares to take a rather great risk. The project represents a rather large risk for the online traffic to *Fædrelandsvennen*.

(Steiro, interview with author, 2023)

Streamlining, New Digital Business Models, and Global Ambitions 73

The complex dynamic between Schibsted and the newspapers was visible and played out in the five areas discussed during this period of the digital transformation of Schibsted's news media. The dynamic was characterized by a combination of the newspapers' autonomy and decentral decision-making and Schibsted's role as both a supportive and centralizing force.

Online Classifieds and Marketplaces – Worldwide Expansion

While one of Schibsted's two core business area, media houses in Norway and Sweden, faced major cost-cutting and restructuring in the wake of the financial crisis, the other, the international classified advertising operations, experienced the opposite. The latter had, since 2008, been organized in Schibsted Classified Media, and this marked an increased focus on international expansion (Schibsted, 2009b). Schibsted underlined its offensive international approach by stating:

> In 2008 and 2009, when the impact of the financial crisis forced economy-wide scale backs in most of the Western world, Schibsted built on its experience with Blocket and rolled out successful online marketplaces in an array of new countries and markets.
>
> (Schibsted, 2022b: 11)

While the Norwegian classified company, FINN, was not part of Schibsted Classified Media, the Swedish classified company Blocket became part of it. This was problematic for *Aftonbladet*, which had increasingly relied on income from Blocket. Although Schibsted centrally had financed the aquisition of Blocket, the classified operation was controlled by *Aftonbladet* up until then. This change represented a certain "polarization between Schibsted and *Aftonbladet*" (Barland, 2012: 161). With the rapid growth and increased importance of the online classified advertising business area for Schibsted, it became cumbersome and a detour to run Blocket through *Aftonbladet*, and Schibsted decided therefore to move Blocket to the new Schibsted Classified Media (Barland, 2012: 161). While *Aftonbladet* continued to market such online services, the newspaper experienced a major financial loss, as the overall revenues was reduced by SEK 555 million after the reorganization (Barland, 2012: 138). However, another reason for incorporating Blocket in Schibsted Classified Media was the fact that the Blocket concept and technology was the key for the international classified roll-out. In 2009, an important strategic expansion in the Nordics was the launch of the classified advertising site, Tori, in Finland. This was the tenth country, outside of Sweden, that a Blocket version had been launched (Schibsted, 2009b: 6).

Then, in 2010, Schibsted bought the remaining 50 percent of the French classified company, Leboncoin, taking full control of the company, valued

74 *Schibsted*

at EUR 200 million (Schibsted, 2022a). This was a major milestone for the international expansion of Schibsted's online classified advertising business, Rolv Erik Ryssdal, recalls; Ryssdal had been appointed CEO of Schibsted only the year before, coming from the position of CEO of Schibsted Classified Media (2008–2009). In the latter position, Ryssdal had been defining the international strategy for Schibsted's classified operations:

> We gave "full throttle" on classified advertising internationally. One of the most important things I did was in the summer of 2010. We went to France on the French National Day, and I negotiated with the head of the company who owned half of Leboncoin, about buying out Leboncoin. It turned out to be a stroke of luck because the value increase in this company has been very big.
>
> (Ryssdal, interview with author, 2024)

In fact, Aleksander Rosinski argues that the acquisition "has gone down in history as Schibsted's best investment ever," as the total acquisition costs were around EUR 200 million and the value of the company today is EUR 5–6 billion. However, as the earlier acquisition of the Trader Classified Media in 2006 was decisive for turning Schibsted from a Scandinavian to an international company, in terms of both reach and corporate mindset, the deal was also key to the Leboncoin acquisition:

> I think Schibsted could never have done the Leboncoin deal if the company hadn't done the earlier Trader Classified Media transaction. Without the latter deal, Schibsted would not have had the people with the right competence who could prepare and make the basis for the proposed deal and give management sufficient comfort to make such a big decision. 100 million euros was a lot of money for Schibsted, at the time. Furthermore, Schibsted had developed both a methodology for classified expansion, called the Blocket playbook, as well as self-confidence, the necessary talent and organization, to be able to start rolling out what they called the Blocket clones, all over the world, in South America, Asia and Europe.
>
> (Rosinski, interview with author, 2023)

However, as the international expansion of online classified advertising sites continued, it became clear that Schibsted had become a "two-speed company" with two business areas with different strategic priorities – "International Classifieds" globally and "News media" in Norway and Sweden, Sverre Munck argues:

> What happened was that the classified ads companies required investment for them to be successful. The technology was not that complicated, but the marketing budgets became extremely large as global players such as eBay and Naspers became more and more interested in this business. The

Streamlining, New Digital Business Models, and Global Ambitions 75

newspapers' investment projects never yielded as much return as classified advertising. So, in the fight for funds, the newspapers would lose, to a large extent. They were allowed to continue investing but were not substantial amounts.

(Munck, interview with author, 2023)

Schibsted's expansion into the Brazilian market in 2011 is probably the most significant example of how capital-intensive and demanding the international online classified expansion had become for the company. At the time, around half of the Brazilian population had Internet access, and mobile Internet penetration was growing. Schibsted launched the Brazilian classified advertising site, Bomnegocio, and soon found itself in a fierce battle for market leadership against the online classified service OLX, owned by the South African media giant Naspers (Eckblad and Gjernes, 2017).

The overall investments of Schibsted's international online classified advertising operations had grown substantially. In 2012, investments rose to NOK 530, and in 2013, the online classified investments increased to NOK 1 billion, primarily costs toward marketing. Many investors began to worry (Schibsted, 2022a). In 2014, Schibsted invested NOK 1.3 billion in the international classified operations that were in an "investment phase"; yet much of this was spent on the Bomnegocio service in Brazil, as the competition with OLX escalated. While OLX had been the market leader, Schibsted's Bomnegocio overtook OLX in terms of page views and had trebled its number of users in one year. Naspers, also expanding extensively online classified internationally, reportedly spent from March 2013 to March 2014 a total of NOK 2 billion, almost all on marketing, and the Brazilian market was the most capital-intensive (Eckblad and Gjernes, 2017).

The competition in online classifieds in Brazil between Schibsted and Naspers was demanding and also controversial as Naspers had recruited the former chief operating officer of Schibsted's international classified operation, into the positon of head of e-commerce (Hauger, 2014). This was one of the factors hardening the competition between Schibsted and Naspers, according to Rosinski:

> During this period, Schibsted had also recruited people externally. One of these people, who at one point was very high up in the Schibsted system, was recruited by Naspers. This is a South African media group that had invested in China in the late 1990s and succeeded with their early investments in Tencent and become very strong in terms of capital. I suspect that the CEO of Naspers saw that Schibsted was doing well in online classified advertising internationally, and thought maybe Naspers should start doing the same. Naspers decided to start investing and recruited this senior manager from Schibsted's classified international business. He took the playbook with him, so to speak, and Naspers then became a big competitor

76 *Schibsted*

to Schibsted. It did not become such a big competitor in Western Europe, because Schibsted had already strong positions there, but above all in Asia and Latin America. Schibsted had launched in Brazil, and so had Naspers, and this led to a very capital-intensive "war."

(Rosinski, interview with author, 2023)

However, as the international expansion and investments intensified, it became clear that the ownership structure of Schibsted posed certain limitations:

It was very capital intensive. The Tinius Trust was not positive to an expansion of the share capital, because it did not have that much capital, and could thus risk lose its controlling ownership of 26.2% of the share capital.

(Munck, interview with author, 2023)

While the Tinius Trusts ownership and long-term thinking had been an advantage for many years, this changed to some extent as classified expansion became so capital demanding. Rosinski argues:

Schibsted's ownership structure was a great advantage in the 2000s, when you needed long-term stability and not necessarily a lot of capital, but one could argue that it became in a sense a bit of a disadvantage 13, 14 years later, when the company needed more capital to expand faster and invest more in the international classified business. However, to some extent this conundrum was addressed in a good way through some smart JV agreements, for instance with Telenor.

(Rosinski, interview with author, 2023)

The enormous investments in Brazil and other international markets led Schibsted to establish a joint venture with Telenor, the former national Norwegian telecom, now a major international telecom company, in 2013. The joint venture was established in both Brazil and Chile and aimed to contribute to strengthen Schibsted's ability to compete, as Naspers was financially significantly stronger (Schibsted, 2022a). Rosinski, who at the time was the Vice President of Telenor Digital overseeing the joint venture classified business side, argues:

In Telenor, Schibsted got a rich uncle, and this probably made Naspers understand that the company could not win the competition. Later Schibsted/Telenor and Naspers entered into an agreement, which reduced the need for capital investments, and resulted in, among other things, a joint venture in Brazil.

(Rosinski, interview with author, 2023)

In 2014, peace broke out as Naspers reportedly realized it could not win against the Telenor-backed Schibsted (Eckblad and Gjernes, 2017). Schibsted became

Streamlining, New Digital Business Models, and Global Ambitions 77

partner with its main competitor, Naspers, along with Telenor and Singapore Press Holdings, with the aim to develop online classified advertising sites in Asia and Latin America. In the major classified market, Brazil, Bomnegocio and OLX were merged. Naspers owned 50 percent of the new company, while the 50/50 Schibsted/Telenor-owned joint venture, SnT Classifieds, owned the other 50 percent. The marketing costs in Brazil decreased significantly in the wake of this transaction (Schibsted, 2022a). Schibsted and Naspers reportedly divided online classified advertising operations between them in over 20 countries and signed a number of confidential agreements on which territories they would not compete in. On the day the deals were made public, the value of the Schibsted share rose over 33 percent, increasing the value of the company with NOK 13 billion to around NOK 52 billion (Eckblad and Gjernes, 2017). By the end of 2014, Schibsted's classified business, including through joint venture, had expanded to around 30 countries (Schibsted, 2014a). These developments underlined the strong financial position of the international classified operations within Schibsted and its major presence across the world.

The Third Business Area: Growth

While Schibsted in 2009 decided to focus on the two main business areas – news media and international classified advertising – the company also decided to continue a third smaller business area: Growth (Sunde, interview with author, 2024). This third business area emerged in Sweden, as particularly the newspaper *Aftonbladet* had been highly active in investing in and acquiring new digital companies and exploiting the newspaper's massive Internet traffic to market these new companies. This strategy became increasingly important for *Aftonbladet* in the wake of the dot-com crash around 2000 as the newspaper sought to develop income from online initiatives and businesses and invest and acquire new digital companies (Barland, 2012: 137; Byttner, 2012). In the early 2000s, one of these companies benefiting from *Aftonbladet*'s online marketing and traffic was Schibsted's newly acquired online classified company, Blocket. Then, in 2006, having been active in this area for several years, *Aftonbladet* established and started operating Aftonbladet Tilvàxtmedier (Growth media) (Barland, 2012: 135).

The innovative culture in *Aftonbladet* for digital innovation and growth initiatives, and the use the online traffic from *Aftonbladet*, to market and drive traffic toward new companies, became more and more significant. By 2008, Aftonbladet Tilvàxtmedier owned 19 online companies, including Hitta.se, Prisjakt, and Tasteline (Schibsted, 2008). Then, as this activity grew into a more defined business area of size, the company, was changed to Schibsted Tilvàxtmedier (Byttner, 2012).

In 2009, Schibsted Sverige was established and consisted of three units: *Aftonbladet, Svenska Dagbladet*, and Schibsted Tilvàxtmedier. The latter turned from a loss of SEK 42 million in 2008 to an operating profit of SEK 11 million in

78 *Schibsted*

2009 (Schibsted, 2009b). The senior management and board of the new Schibsted Sweden organization (est. 2009) proved vital for the Growth business area. The Growth enthusiast, Raoul Grünthal, was appointed the CEO of Schibsted Sweden and the Board of Schibsted Sweden consisted of representatives from the two media houses, *Aftonbladet* and *Svenska Dagbladet* and Tilväxtmedier. This emphasized the strong position of the digital growth and venture activity within Schibsted Sweden. Schibsted Tilväxtmedier focused particularly on investing in and acquiring online companies within finance technology, or fintech, and personal finance. In 2009, the company bought shares in the Swedish online consumer loan company, Lendo. The company became a main point of reference for Schibsted when presenting its growth investments in the following years. Then in 2010, as Schibsted Tilväxtmedier in Sweden had developed and acquired several growth online companies and services, Schibsted Growth was established in Norway as well (Schibsted, 2022a).

In Sweden, the invention of the "Trafikfonden" (the "Traffic fund") became a tool that systematized the practice of using the major Internet traffic generated by *Aftonbladet* and Blocket to promote and market new online companies and services, Raoul Grünthal, then CEO of Schibsted Sverige, points out:

> In Sweden, we then built a fund, "Trafikfonden", where everyone who was part of the fund also had to contribute. As I recall, everyone contributed two percent of their turnover to the fund, and at the same time, we from Schibsted Sweden centrally also contributed. The money went back to those who sent the most traffic to others, that is mainly *Aftonbladet* and Blocket. It was important for building value within the group, but it was also important symbolically and communicatively. The signal was: "Here we collaborate and build value together for the future. If you want to run your own silos the old-fashioned way, you can do it at Bonnier or elsewhere, but here we do it this way." Collaboration was in our DNA.
>
> (Grünthal, interview with author, 2024)

A key point, Grünthal argues, was that newspapers should be central in creating value and growth, not only from online subscriptions and advertising but also by leveraging online traffic in the marketing of new ideas, ventures, and companies. Schibsted exported the concept of the Trafikfonden from Sweden to Schibsted in Norway, around 2010. The Trafikfonden was an innovation relevant for both journalism and market expansion, Gard Steiro, Chief Editor and CEO of the Norwegian newspaper, *VG*, argues:

> There are two arguments for doing this, journalistically. One is that it makes sense to show people more relevant content from another medium (within Schibsted), and the other is that there was suddenly some form of value in doing so. However, what is really the value in this for Schibsted is the

Streamlining, New Digital Business Models, and Global Ambitions 79

marketing power. You can build up new services by using the marketing power of the big traffic engines *VG* and *Aftonbladet.*

(Steiro, interview with author, 2023)

By 2012, Sweden Tilväxtmedier owned over 20 Internet-based companies, particularly within personal finance. Schibsted claimed that these companies "benefit greatly from the strong traffic positions and brands of Schibsted's established operations in Sweden" (Schibsted, 2012). In 2013, Schibsted Tilväxtmedier changed its name to Schibsted Growth, and in 2014, Schibsted Growth consisted of growth and venture activities not only in Sweden but also in Norway and France, as Schibsted Growth became part of Raoul Grünthal's, the CEO of Schibsted Sweden, portfolio (Schibsted, 2014b). In fact, in 2014, Schibsted Growth was established as a third division of Schibsted alongside the media houses and online classified businesses (Schibsted, 2014a: 3).

Conclusion

Throughout the period between 2009 and 2014, the external, company, and leadership dimensions shaped and influenced the corporate strategies and the operationalization as Schibsted digital transformation and international expansion gathered speed.

In terms of the external dimensions, major upheavals took place in the media market. Facebook and Google expanded rapidly, the financial crisis hit Schibsted hard, advertising revenues dropped, and major divestments in non-core businesses and the cost-cutting in news media were implemented. The phase is characterized by the focusing on the core business areas, news media and online classified, with the consolidation and intensified search for business model within news media and the intensified international expansion of the online classified advertising operations. The corporate strategy in this phase exemplifies how financial recessions and crises lead to changes in resource allocations and innovation (Doyle, 2013).

In terms of the leadership dimension, Kjell Aamot left in 2009 after over 20 years as CEO of Schibsted, and the new CEO of Schibsted, Rolv Erik Ryssdal, with long operational background as CEO of the international classified businesses and CEO of both *Aftonbladet* and *Aftenposten*, took the reign. Birger Magnus, Deputy CEO of Schibsted and Executive Vice President since 1996, and central in the digital transformation of particualrly the Schibsted's news media and the development of its corporate and organizational culture, left the company after around 13 years. These changes led to several changes in how the company was run and its strategy. While Aamot encouraged diversification and experimentation, and let the senior executives operate independently to a large degree, in the wake of the financial crisis, Ryssdal launched a new strategy focusing on the two core business areas: news media and online classifieds

80 *Schibsted*

internationally, as well as the smaller, emerging digital growth and venture initiative – becoming formally a third part of the company later. However, in this phase, the problematic side of the relation between two core businesses became more evident. Investments in international classified expansion were prioritized and require enormous sums as this market was maturing and competition intensifies, while media had less financial potential and was hard hit by cost-cutting and received less investment. This highlights the "Agent-Principal Problem" within Schibsted (Artero and Manfredi, 2016: 53). The new CEO of Schibsted, Rolv Erik Ryssdal, aimed to align the company's corporate strategy with investors that consider international classified advertising as the most attractive investment, while at the same time there is a need to balance this approach with Tinius Trust, the largest owner, which has its focus on news media, as defined in its Articles of Association.

In terms of company dimensions, the ownership form became an issue when operationalizing the costly strategy of expanding classified internationally. Capital raising through the issuing of new stocks was challenging, as the Tinius Trust had to buy shares to maintain its ownership part. This points to a general weakness of trust or foundation ownership of news media in the Nordic region, as their holdings cannot be easily diluted, and this may limit growth and expansion (Achtenhagen et al., 2018: 147). In this phase, Schibsted's media increasingly focused on coordination and collaboration between the news media businesses, much due to the costs of digitization. This led to developments that culminated in Schibsted taking full ownership over several regional newspapers in Norway, gathering them in the company Media Norge (est. 2009), which is later expanded into the larger Schibsted Norge (est. 2012), that included all its Norwegian media houses as well as FINN, the national classified advertising company. Similarly, Schibsted Sweden (est. 2009) included the company's media holdings and Blocket, the national classified advertising company. However, Schibsted's consolidations were criticized by both competitors and media and competition authorities for their possible threat to media diversity and for its considerable market power.

The establishment of these major national news and classified companies also gives insight into the dynamic between centralization and autonomy: between the Schibsted group, and the individual companies within these new structures. Consolidation within the news sector is seen as a common strategic trend also among news companies, and large media companies are able to benefit from economies of scale (Lindberg, 2023). However, many of the initiatives for cost-cutting and collaboration, leading to this consolidation, were not at first initiated centrally by Schibsted but by its newspapers. They saw the need to act as the future financial projections in the digital market were dramatic. Schibsted supported these initiatives, but within some of the newspapers, it was difficult to comprehend the causality of the various, parallel processes and contributed to some resentment toward Schibsted centrally. Still, the consolidation of the newspapers was made possible much due to a new generation of editors and

Streamlining, New Digital Business Models, and Global Ambitions 81

CEOs of the newspapers, who saw the need for closer collaboration between the companies and across areas including technology, editorial, advertising, and in-house competence. The cost-cutting also led to the sacking of employees in the newspapers, but this also opened for the hiring people with much needed digital competence in journalism and technology. This exemplifies a shift in relation to corporate culture in the digital era, as new norms that guide how work is done and organized emerges (Golnaz Sadri and Lees, 2001: 853)

Several forms of innovations underpin developments in both media and classified advertising in this phase. The policy of establishing new companies outside the main company continued, that is *VGTV* and *VG Mobil*. These new companies are given resources and autonomy and a remit to experiment and develop a sustainable business model, before being integrated in the mother company, in this case, the *VG* newspaper. Through organizational or structural ambidexterity, digital innovation and business development was done in separate units or companies, before being incorporated in the company when deemed strong enough (Harland, 2018: 3). This way of organizing the new digital business areas contributed to the development of a corporate culture, and a more distinct online journalism, separate from the main legacy newspaper. A major innovation breakthrough was the development of online user payment and subscription business model for newspapers. The user-payment solution were developed in-house by the smallest newspaper, *Fædrelandsvennen*, in 2012, and was then rolled out across the other Schibsted newspapers.The international classified expansion was made possible much due to the acquisition of the Swedish online classified advertising site, Blocket. Its innovative concept and disruptive business model was further developed and tailored to the different international markets. The establishment of the Trafikfonden (the Traffic fund), represented an important innovation, first in Sweden and then in Norway, as new Schibsted companies benefited from being part of an ecosystem in which the large online newspapers or classified sites utilized their major Internet traffic to market and promote them.

5 In the Face of Global Platformization: The Ecosystem Strategy

2014–2017

As Schibsted's print newspaper revenues reached a dramatic low in the mid-2010s, and digital revenues did not compensate for this loss, the company also faced intensified competition from the global platforms Google and Facebook for advertising, including classified advertising, as well as increasingly also in terms of news distribution. While Facebook's features for sharing and recommending news items were viewed by many in the news industry as an opportunity, it was also troubling as publishers began to lose control over the distribution of its content. This competition accentuated as platforms began releasing news-related features and products, thus increasingly becoming news destinations themselves. Media companies, media authorities, politicians, and other stakeholders in Schibsted's home markets, Norway and Sweden, feared the consequences of this development on the business sustainability and future of news media. Many Nordic news media companies responded by collaborating with the global platforms to develop their business models, while Schibsted chose to create its own platforms. Around 2014, Schibsted launched the ambitious "Ecosystem strategy," focusing on developing company-wide platforms in its two core business areas, news media and online classified advertising, to counter the global platforms. This marked a major shift in strategy, as the focus on data science, audience analytics, and identity-based ecosystems and the global scaling of products and technology were now the key. This strategy also represented Schibsted at its most centralized, as it aimed for a new matrix organization across the company. A key question was how this ambitious, technology-focused "One company" strategy would fare, facing Schibsted's tradition of decentralized decision-making both through editorial autonomy and company culture, and the highly successful international online classified advertising sites developing independently within diverse national media markets and contexts.

The Ecosystem and Platform Strategy: A Fundamental Corporate Strategic Shift

In 2013, the Nieman Journalism Lab, published an article warning of serious consequences for news companies in the digital domain, also in the Nordic region:

DOI: 10.4324/9781003439431-5

In the Face of Global Platformization: The Ecosystem Strategy 83

"It is the Googles, Microsoft's, Facebooks, Twitters, and Yahoos who have built their own data advantages, based both on huge usage and investment in analytics" (Doctor, 2013). In contrast, news companies, including Schibsted, which is considered a digital pioneer and innovator internationally, were described as lagging and playing catch-up. Sverre Munck, EVP, and central to the digital transformation and internationalization at Schibsted since 1994, acknowledged that "[o]ur analytics were haphazard, ad-hoc, case-by-case" (Munck quoted in Doctor, 2013). In 2013, a reorganization of Schibsted's senior executive and leadership group market the beginning of the company's new corporate strategy of establishing data ecosystems and platforms, through data science and analytics, and data-driven products, across the company. In October 2013, Sverre Munck retired after 20 years in various senior executive and strategic roles in Schibsted. In his place Frode Eilertsen was hired as Executive Vice President of strategy and digital transformation, responsible for the Schibsted group's corporate strategy development (Schibsted, 2013). Soon after, Edoardo Jacucci, was hired as VP of strategy and data analytics (Schibsted, 2014a). Both Eilertsen and Jacucci had previously been McKinsey consultants. Then, Rian Liebenberg, former Google executive was hired as Group Chief Technology Officer (CTO), and Adam Kinney, formerly at Google and Twitter, was hired as head of data science at Schibsted (Schibsted, 2014c, 2014d). Frode Eilertsen, EVP of digital transformation and CEO of Schibsted product and technology (2013–2016), the part of Schibsted to lead the operationalization of the ecosystem and platform strategy, together with Rian LiebenBerg, CTO, took charge. Eilertsen argued strongly for news publishers' need to build ecosystems and platforms themselves, just as Google and Facebook had done (Eilertsen, 2015).

News Media

Schibsted's Norwegian and Swedish media houses had in the years around 2010 been through a process of increased integration, collaboration, and coordination of its editorial and advertising operations, and investments, particularly in technology. At the time of the development of the ecosystem strategy, Roaul Grüthal was the CEO of Schibsted Sweden and Didrik Munch was the CEO of Schibsted Norge:

> I was positive and one of the instigators, because I thought we were moving much too slowly. There was a very strong identity linked to the news brands, but then we started with these matrix organizations, making people responsible for advertising and the user market and all technology across the brands.
>
> (Munch, interview with author, 2024)

This marked the start of the implementation of the ecosystem in response to the global platform giants' expansion. Already by 2014, Google and Facebook's

84 *Schibsted*

income from the Norwegian and Swedish advertising market had increased dramatically. In the second quarter of 2014, Schibsted lost between 17 and 18 percent year-on-year in advertising revenue in the subscription newspapers, and the total advertising income from online and print fell by 14 percent. At the time, Google and Facebook had already a NOK 3 billion share of the total Norwegian advertising market of NOK 20 billion (Bisgaard, 2014). The global giants were able to collect and utilize user data to create more targeted and efficient advertising products than Schibsted, Siv Juvik Tveitnes, current CEO of Schibsted Media, argues:

> What happens from 2015/2016 in the advertising market is important. Now the global platforms have entered. They are incredibly large, with enormous distribution power, both Facebook and Google. With lots of data they create effective, good advertising products, while we still have *VG* here and FINN here and *Bergens Tidende* here, which are partly small competitors in a common advertising market.
>
> (Juvik Tveitnes, interview with author, 2024)

The global giants had not only a competitive and technological advantage over Schibsted and the other media companies but also benefited from being "digital zero taxpayers," by not paying tax in Norway, as their main offices were outside the country (Tobiassen and Ovrebo Johannessen, 2014). The worry was that Schibsted could end up being completely dominated by, particularly, Google. Already in the mid-1990s, during Schibsted early forays into the digital domain, the company had been conscious not to let the expanding international companies become gatekeepers between Schibsted's content, audience, and advertising. This policy and strategy could now be challenged by, particularly, Google:

> We saw the platforms emerge, both within search and community, and launched our own sites, Sesam within search and Nettby as a community site. Our instinct was to compete and defend our position. We reckoned it would be difficult, but thought we could have a fair chance since Norwegian was an insignificant language and we had direct access to the newspaper archives. Rolv Erik (Ryssdal) and I discussed how to react when Google launch its ad platform. Should we develop our own or should we join the crowd and go with Google. We decided to build our own. My thinking was that either we succeed and defend our position, or we will be in a much better position to negotiate terms. We did not want to be pushed to the back seat and leave the customer interface to Google ending up as a vassal or sub supplier. Then our content could be commoditized. It was clear to me that keeping direct contact with customers was key in the digital economy.
>
> (Sunde, interview with author, 2024)

In the Face of Global Platformization: The Ecosystem Strategy 85

Rolv Erik Ryssdal, CEO of Schibsted at the time, argues: "If we have good technology expertise, then we have such good data about advertisers and consumers, especially in Norway and Sweden, that we can build an ecosystem that is stronger than what others have" (Ryssdal, interview with author, 2024, author's translation). However, to compete with Google and Facebook, the Schibsted's news businesses would have to combine, coordinate, pool resources further, and achieve benefits of scale in terms of technology investments and be able to create competitive advertising products, Gard Steiro, Chief Editor and CEO of *VG*, argues:

> Around 2015, a couple of things happen. Firstly, one is beginning to be uncertain about the entire digital business model for advertisements. Then, Facebook really have come in and started to take large market shares, but also Google. You really start to notice that social media is coming in. They have existed for a few years, but now they have become very large in the advertising market. So, the digital growth *VG* has had suddenly stops. In discussions in the Schibsted group management, people are beginning to think that the newspapers are not big enough on their own. The investments you have to make on the technology side are so large that even *VG* or *Aftonbladet* cannot do this alone. There is everything from infrastructure to innovation to absolutely everything. So, while the regional newspapers and *Aftenposten*, at that time, already have a good number of joint services and have built up a lot in common, now you go in and start building the platforms.
>
> (Steiro, interview with author, 2023)

Sondre Gravir, the then EVP of Schibsted Europe Established Sites, part of the international online classified advertising operations, and member of the Schibsted leadership group, underlines the severity of the situation:

> The individual newspaper alone could not compete against the large, national and eventually the international advertising giants for the digital advertising money in the Norwegian market. So, you had to join forces across regional media houses, because the competition was intensifying.
>
> (Gravir, interview with author, 2024)

Facebook, as well as Google, did not only represent major competition for advertising but also in terms of distribution of news content and consumers. Google News had already launched news aggregators in Norway and Sweden by the mid-2000s, and one of Schibsted's responses was its own search engine, Sesam, in 2005, closely tied to the newspaper, *VG* (Anand and Hood, 2007: 16). Google News's reception was mixed in the region, and the aim of Sesam was to give users a better overview and insight in news online, with a particular local focus, through "local search," that is the

86 *Schibsted*

"crawling" of Norwegian online sites, and access proprietary media content, archives, and directories (Schibsted, 2006a: 47). However, Google proved a far superior competitor in all respects, and Sesam closed in 2009: "We wanted a share of the pie but underestimated our ability to compete with Google," Rolv Erik Ryssdal argued (Ryssdal quoted in Aldridge Lynum, 2014, author's translation).

In 2006, the largest Schibsted-owned newspaper, *VG*, launched Nettby in Norway. At its height, Nettby had more than 350,000 daily users, 800,000 registered user profiles, and more than 70 percent of Norwegian teenagers had created a profile. However, from around 2008, the service experienced a continuous decline in activity. Despite the implementation of a range of measures to turn things around, the competition from Facebook was too great, and Nettby closed in 2010. This was a general trend among national social media services internationally (Mjos, 2012).

As Facebook expanded globally, a complex relationship with legacy news media evolved. Facebook became increasingly a major competitor for legacy news media as news and information destination. At the same time, many legacy news media adopted and utilized the social media platform to distribute its own news content. The competition was to intensify further with the launch of news-related products such as Facebook Instant Articles (2015), Facebook Live (2016), the video-on-demand product, Facebook Watch (2017), and later Facebook news (2019), also within the service's ecosystem (Nielsen and Ganter, 2022: 2).

Classified International

By late 2014, Schibsted's online classified advertising operation had expanded to around 30 countries and the company aimed to become a global leader within this business area (Schibsted, 2014a). The rationale for creating a global platform for classified business mirrored the one for the media business side, Sondre Gravir, the then head of Schibsted Europe Established classified operations, argues:

> Exactly the same analogy describes the situation in the marketplaces. You had wonderful marketplace companies that had been allowed to run very independently. You had built up Leboncoin in France, Subito in Italy and so on. They had started with the same technology platform (Blocket) and the same product at the bottom. But, as there had been no coordination, these classified companies had moved in completely different directions. And that was probably also the source of their success, because you could be very local, you could adapt to local competition, and to the local user preferences. But, parallel to that, large international giants emerged as we know, Facebook, Google and so on, which take a lot of the advertising revenue, which take a lot of the attention. You had Facebook Marketplaces which

In the Face of Global Platformization: The Ecosystem Strategy 87

instead of the local adaptation, had an international product, thus being able to put large technology investments into that product. There is always a balance between being global and extracting cross-horizontal synergies, versus being local and only focusing on one market.

(Gravir, interview with author, 2024)

Former SVP International Marketplaces, and current CEO of Schibsted Marketplaces, Christian Printzell Halvorsen, elaborates on the challenge facing Schibsted:

At the time, we had marketplaces in 25–30 countries, which were all running separately. That structure made it difficult to innovate quickly, so we thought we had to create more scale in terms of technology both for the marketplaces and for the media. As a result, we established a strong joint technology organization and recruited many incredibly competent people.

(Printzell Halvorsen, interview with author, 2024)

To remain competitive and grow in the international online classified market, the ideal was for Schibsted to create a common technology platform across its different international sites (Gravir, interview with author, 2024).

The Operationalization of the Ecosystem and Platform Strategy: Media and Classifieds

Schibsted embarked on the implementation of the ecosystem strategy, technology cooperation, and development of platforms across the company and its core business areas: news media and online classified advertising. In 2014, Schibsted established an office in London, with hubs in Oslo, Stockholm, Barcelona, and Krakow, with the aim to strengthen the company's product and technology development. Schibsted increased its in-house tech competence dramatically (Schibsted, 2015a). In less than two years, from 2014 to 2016, Schibsted hired 500 tech staff, and in total had 1,400 developers across the business areas: online classified, news media, as well as the growth and venture business side. London was the main hub, overseeing the other technology development hubs, that worked closely with the different brands in over 30 countries (WAN-IFRA, 2017).

The operationalization of the ecosystem strategy proved costly, along with the continuing investment needs within its core business areas, and particularly international classified expansion. Therefore, in 2015, Schibsted decided to split its share into A and B shares, where the B share had one-tenth of the voting rights. While it was controversial among certain shareholders, it was approved at the annual general meeting, and the company raised NOK 2.6 billion through issuing new B shares to investor (Schibsted, 2022a). The issuing of the B shares was a way of preventing Tinius Trust's ownership from becoming diluted when raising

88   *Schibsted*

capital. In this way, the Tinius Trust's retained a 25.1 percent ownership and 26 percent of the voting rights in the company and thereby also the negative controlling rights over the company. While the number of A shares normally remain stable over time, B shares were to be used as a source for financing growth, acquisitions, and investments (Schibsted, 2015c: 89, 168; Mossin, 2015).

As Schibsted reorganized to focus on data-driven ecosystems and platforms cutting across the company's four geographies – Schibsted Norway, Schibsted Sweden, Schibsted Europe Established, and Schibsted Emerging Markets – centralization was at its strongest within the company. The year 2015, the company argued, was "a turning point in Schibsted's organizational development where the Group pivots from a largely decentralized structure to a matrix organization" (Schibsted, 2015c: 40). The current CEO of Schibsted Media, Siv Juvik Tveitnes, recalls:

> Schibsted makes a very big investment, and builds up the Product and Technology organization, and reorganize Schibsted in line with a vision that we will create "One Company," and that, especially on the product and technology side, will build common platforms across the company.
>
> (Juvik Tveitnes, interview with author, 2024)

Chief Editor and CEO of *VG*, Gard Steiro, agrees:

> This is the period when CEO Rolv Erik Ryssdal, at a large meeting of managers, says: 'Now we are 'One company'. Schibsted is no longer a 'House of Brands,' we are 'One Company'. We must work together to lift this.'
>
> (Steiro, interview with author, 2023)

To support the new Schibsted group organization and implementation of this strategy, new leadership principles were created with the contribution from 70 managers across the group. The principles were set of attitudes and behaviors that aimed to develop a "strong Schibsted culture across the Group" with a "a shared common view of the business," and aiming to "drive change in a matrix organization" (Schibsted, 2015c: 40).

Terje Seljeseth, the first CEO of FINN and EVP chief product officer from 2015, was for a time in charge of the work on developing a global online classified advertising platform across the different international online classified sites. The ideal was to create one global platform for all the classified sites, similar to Google and Facebook:

> I took over the responsibility of building global platforms across all these companies, and then we hired someone called Rian Liebenberg, who came from Google originally. We established international teams in Barcelona, London, Stockholm and Oslo to create scalable platform modules that could be used by everyone instead of everything being made over again

In the Face of Global Platformization: The Ecosystem Strategy 89

in 20 countries. The idea behind this was to make it once somewhere, state-of-the-art, and then spread it out. It was a good idea, but difficult to implement.

(Seljeseth, interview with author, 2024)

In the autumn of 2016, Rian Liebenberg, Chief Technology Officer, and the company's most senior tech executive, presented the new, global organization to the financial market, its shareholders, and finance analytics. The Schibsted organization Schibsted Products and Technology was, reportedly, to develop components that could be reused and enable scaling of platforms for all media and classified advertising operations in Schibsted, aiming to increase the speed and efficiency of the implementation of the ecosystem strategy (Eckblad, 2018). However, a major challenge was the fact that Schibsted's classified sites internationally were a mix of different technologies: Blocket, in particular, but some were based on Finn, and others were based on existing local platforms, Seljeseth recalls:

Schibsted used several technology platforms and that was part of the problem. If we had had one platform that we used everywhere, it would have been much easier to do the globalization of platform development, but we had a whole bunch of different platforms to deal with. So, trying to streamline and make it more like Google and Facebook, that have global platform development for all countries, it was an extremely complicated matter.

(Seljeseth, interview with author, 2024)

Within news media, in 2015, the situation was different. The Swedish newspaper, *Svenska Dagbladet*, was the first to launch their newsroom on the new Schibsted Media Platform (SMP) – a "group-wide publishing tool" for all the Schibsted-owned media houses. Parts of the platform had already been taken up by all of Schibsted's newspapers in Sweden and Norway (Schibsted, 2015b). While *VG* TV had launched in 2013, in 2015, a video platform was launched for the other newspapers to use. Then, in 2016, the SMP, the shared news platform, for the creation and distribution, and monetization of content, was rolled out in the media houses, with the Norwegian *VG*, being the last newspaper to do so (Schibsted, 2022a; WAN-IFRA, 2017).

The media business area managed to create a common platform for editorial news in both Norway and Sweden. In Norway, the ability to do so should also be seen in light of the earlier collaboration between Schibsted wholly and co-owned newspapers in advertising sales in the last half of the 1990s, but not least also through the formal establishment of Media Norge and Schibsted Norge, in 2009 and 2012, respectively. This contributed to enable a centralized process where developers, around 100, from all the media houses contributed to building the news platform, with all reporting to the same management, the centralized Schibsted Products and Technology organization (Schibsted, 2017).

90 *Schibsted*

Siv Juvik Tveitnes, CEO of Schibsted Media, points out that such technology had to be developed in-house:

> During this period, we drew up an architecture for how we would build a common editorial platform for all our editorial offices. It goes without saying that the way we tell our stories digitally is very different from what we have done in print. There were no systems out there that we could use, so we were probably early to understand those needs, and then gathered most of our common product and technology people to build a common platform. We started with that in 2015, as I remember.
>
> (Juvik Tveitnes, interview with author, 2024)

In 2017, the work on the SMP focused on further integration of all the different technologies in the media houses into one shared stack to enable the sharing of technology solutions developed in one media house with the others. While the platform was the same for all newspapers, it was possible to tailor their appearance (Schibsted, 2017).

In 2015/2016, parallel to the SMP, the development of a common advertising sales organization started – first for the media houses in Sweden, then in Norway. Again, this group-wide approach to creating an advertising platform was a response to Google and Facebook's inroads in the advertising market in the region. Siv Juvik Tveitnes explains:

> The global giants were of course there, and they took market shares all the time, but we started talking about us being a joint force and able to collaborate on advertising. When it comes to the ecosystem, advertisements are perhaps the area where we have really succeeded and where we have a strong joint force in both the Swedish and Norwegian markets, and we see in the years that followed that it was a big job to create a common strategy, get the people to believe in it, and that everyone had to give up something of their own domain and lean into a community. It was a big job on the systems side to get common systems and a common operating strategy out to the customers. We started with that quite early on and were the first to have that strategy. And then we see that other media groups, such as Amedia and Bonnier, have copied it.
>
> (Juvik Tveitnes, interview with author, 2024)

Christian Printzell Halvorsen, former SVP for International Classified and current CEO of Schibsted Marketplaces, argues that the limited financial resources created a situation in which media houses had a more shared understanding of the need to cooperate particularly in technology; yet there were limits to how far one could centralize:

> The media part of Schibsted has always had tighter finances, and when you have that, it is clear that there are some underlying driving forces that drive you toward more synergies and joint technology solutions. There has been a

In the Face of Global Platformization: The Ecosystem Strategy 91

little less of that in the marketplace part. At the same time, editorial responsibility is very central in our media. Fortunately, I must say. However, that editorial responsibility adds up to a very strong autonomy in the local media, whether it is *VG, Aftenposten* or *Bergens Tidende*, which makes it difficult to fully centralize. And in the marketplaces, that I know well, we have had a very good economy, which has led to less pressure and underlying driving forces that move in the direction of synergies and joint solutions.

(Printzell Halvorsen, interview with author, 2024)

Still, Schibsted's consolidated news companies, first Media Norge (est. 2009), Schibsted Sverige (est. 2009), and then Schibsted Norge (est. 2012), were all created to achieve synergies and economies of scale. The strategic mergers were criticized for the possible negative effect of such centralization on media diversity and editorial independence, as leading national and regional newspapers became more closely integrated. In the mid-2010s, two news content analyses of these newspapers point to a more nuanced development. While a consolidation in editorial content in lifestyle and sports was found, among the regional newspapers, a "differentiation strategy remains important to secure local identity, and hence loyal audiences" (Sjøvaag, 2014: 519). In terms of editorial independence and media diversity, user payment was also an issue. Yet an early study of these newspapers suggested that the local content was restricted to subscribers, while syndicated content and breaking news were also open to readers who are not subscribers. The latter generated Internet traffic and visitors, while the former represented the "most valued" news content and was placed behind the paywall (Sjøvaag, 2015: 305).

Parts of the news sector internationally considered the emergence of Facebook and Google as a major opportunity to also reach people who not often access news via the news companies' online sites. Most news companies have in some way a presence within and a relation to the social media services ecosystems, yet many news publishers have a fear of becoming too reliant on these powerful platforms that are outside their control (Nielsen and Ganter, 2022: 9). This points to a key consequence of the wider process of platformization, namely "platform-dependency" also within news and cultural production (Poell et al., 2021). While Schibsted decided to create in-house platforms for media and advertising in the mid-2010, other large Norwegian newspaper companies, such as Aller and Amedia, at the time decided to form business relationships with the global platforms within both distribution and advertising (Ihlebæk and Sundet, 2021: 2192). The Aller-owned Norwegian national newspaper, *Dagbladet*, for example, a relatively small media player with limited recourses, decided on such a pragmatic strategy, establishing a close business relationship with Google for digital products and services (Eide and Myrvang, 2018).

Schibsted's decision to avoid such relations in the digital era can be traced back to the mid-1990s, when Schibsted built the Internet portal *Scandinavia Online*, to be a first mover in the Nordic region, and prevent international companies from becoming gatekeepers for news content, advertising, and readers

92 *Schibsted*

(Munck, interview with author, 2023). However, Schibsted's decision and principle has also been explained by its major market share and ability to leverage size and economies of scale. In the wake of the financial crisis, the consolidation of five newspapers and its national online classified adverting giant, FINN, through Schibsted Norge strengthened Schibsted's market position and turned it into a much stronger competitor in the newspaper market (Aller 2, quoted in Ihlebæk and Sundet, 2021: 2192). Schibsted has had a market advantage that contributed to enabling the creation of its media and advertising platforms. An executive at Aller pointed out, at the time: "Schibsted is one of the biggest media houses in Europe and developed solutions to avoid cooperation with Google. We had to choose a different path" (Aller 1, quoted in Ihlebæk and Sundet, 2021: 2192).

The Challenges of Creating a Global Classified Platform

The development of the ambitious global online classified platform and common technology solutions proved to be complex and challenging. In theory, there were two alternatives when embarking on this task. Either building one classified platform from scratch or by gradually introducing new building blocks or modules in existing classified platforms that communicate with each other. Schibsted first attempted to go for the former – creating one, new platform. Ole Jacob Sunde, explains,

> In global tech companies, products usually take priority over geography. This entails that the profit responsibility stays with the product management and the country leadership and country profitability will be subordinated. You will always have to make regional adjustments, but they are kept to a minimum and the platform serves a global market. In this model you could reap substantial scale effects and centralize the major product development decisions. We recognized this in Schibsted and began the "Rocket" project. The ambition was to build a unified standard classified site for alle the countries in which we operated. But the project did not fly.
>
> (Sunde, interview with author, 2024)

There are several reasons for why it was challenging to create a common technology platform for the international classified sites. One of them was that this development did not start from scratch. Sondre Gravir, then head of Schibsted Europe Established Marketplaces, explains:

> One approach was that you could imagine that you would create a completely new, independent product from scratch, and that was what was then called "Rocket." Then, you can see how far you got with this approach and see if you could replace the technology platforms in some of these markets with this new product. The alternative is to take the building block method, to speak in figuratively language. A good technology platform consists of

In the Face of Global Platformization: The Ecosystem Strategy   93

separate modules that talk to each other. A bad technology platform is spaghetti code that hangs together and is impossible to untangle. So, then you also started making these platforms in the different markets more modular, and then you start with what you called "Schibsted common components." We start by changing one module at a time. So, there are different approaches. Either you take it gradually or you do it through a "big bang," with a new product, which was then called "Rocket." Then, we concluded after a period, that: "No, it is better to do it modularly, step by step."

(Gravir, interview with author, 2024)

In 2017, towards the end of the period when attempting to building a global online classified platform and ecosystem, the then CEO of Schibsted, Rolv Erik Ryssdal, acknowledged that, when trying to exert "more central influence, that affects the role of local management. . . . [T]hat is the big challenge that we are going through now" (Ryssdal quoted in WAN-IFRA, 2017). This points to the dynamic between centralization and decentralization that proved too complex for Schibsted to succeed in developing a global platform for the international online classified sites. Christian Printzell Halvorsen, former SVP International Marketplaces and current CEO of Schibsted Marketplaces, explains:

I sat in the middle of it. I moved to Barcelona and helped establish the technology hub there. So, I have painfully experienced this and felt it on my body. We didn't make it. The main reason was that we did not succeed in getting the people in the local companies onboard in both the media and the marketplaces. There was a lot of friction and tug-of-war between the centralized technology and product environment and the local organizations. In the end, that tug-of-war became so powerful and so conflict-oriented that we had to turn around and go back, and reverse part of the joint technology initiative and investment.

(Printzell Halvorsen, interview with author, 2024)

Many of the national classified sites were not compatible with the global technology functions developed, but the failure to succeed was also due to the lack of will and motivation of the directors of the individual international online classified sites. These sites had developed autonomously with success and within a specific media market context, Sunde explains:

The Blocket code was easily adaptable to local markets. This enabled us to move quickly and launch in many countries in parallel. Local management could decide the tweaks and ad-ons which were key in conquering the number one position in their market. We avoided head office bureaucracy and remained agile to local demands. This strategy led us to gain market dominance in market after market. However, the weakness was that the sites' base technology gradually deviated in structure to a point where new features were difficult to introduce. We lost the scale advantage of being

94 *Schibsted*

big. The decentralized structure also hampered the introduction of our own ad platform. Our country managers were hesitant to taking on new and untested technology when they could stay with market leading platforms like Google. We were struggling to get buy in. Remember that Schibsted was decentralized according to geography and the profitability responsibility stayed with the country manager not the product manager.

(Sunde, interview with author, 2024)

Another reason for the failure to develop the global online classified advertising platform was the impact of the implementation of a new organization of Scchibsted in a matrix structure. This involved collaboration across brands and countries with new technology with people who did not know each other and this complicated the coordination. This was very much in contrast to the way Schibsted traditionally was organized and its work culture, emphasizing fast decision-making, trust, and flexibility; Rolv Erik Ryssdal, the CEO of Schibsted at the time, and responsible for the ecosystem strategy, explains:

The idea may be good, but it turned out that our ability to implement it was not good enough, because we had a relatively decentralized structure. People were used to making quick decisions. I remember writing a separate memo to my own management group, where I asked: are we about to freeze? Because what happened was that people thought that we should cooperate better across the various countries and the new technology department in London, and between people who didn't know each other very well. So, instead of having a culture where quick decisions could be made, we instead prioritized achieving synergy effects on technology, but that required a lot of coordination across the group. There were complicated matrix organizations, that Schibsted did not have experience in. As the CEO, I take the responsibility, even though both the board and the management group agreed that this was an excellent idea. Yet, we had no experience working in that type of organization. People became confused and a little paralyzed, and then decisions took much longer instead of us being able to connect the various nodes more quickly. So, we had to back down on this.

(Ryssdal, interview with author, 2024)

The two most senior tech executives tasked with leading the implementation of Schibsted's ecosystem and platform strategy soon left the company. Already in 2016, Frode Eilertsen left Schibsted, after three years as EVP of digital transformation and CEO of Schibsted's product and technology. Two years later, he was followed by Rian Liebenberg, Chief Platform officer.

Conclusion

In the phase, 2014 to 2017, of Schibsted's digital transformation and international expansion, the dynamic between centralization and decentralization took

In the Face of Global Platformization: The Ecosystem Strategy 95

new forms. These are mapped out by examining the external, leadership, and company dimensions that shape and influence the corporate strategies and the operationalization of them.

In terms of external dimensions, the market situation changed dramatically, the combination of Google and Facebook taking larger and larger market shares of advertising, the shifting user patterns and dramatic drop in print newspaper advertising and further pressure to cut costs in media meant that Schibsted decided to go head to head with the global platforms launching their own ecosystem and platform strategy. Schibsted had, particularly in Sweden, used the term ecosystem for its collaboration between its companies, particularly in using established companies and their Internet traffic, such as *Aftonbladet*, to market and promote new digital companies. However, in this phase, Schibsted's company-wide ecosystem strategy referred to the development of data-driven ecosystems that aimed to cut across its business areas, companies, and brands. This exemplified the popularity, yet often ambiguous nature and unclear definition of the concept of ecosystem (Kostovska et al., 2020; Doyle, 2022). In terms of media system, in this phase, the public debate on the impact and consequences of the expansion of the global platforms intensified in the region. Now, global, regional, national, and local media companies competed for advertising revenue and the time of users (Mjøs, 2022). A problematic side of the global giant's entry was their role as digital intermediaries within the national media landscape (Westlund et al., 2020). Schibsted is a vocal public critic of the global giants and positions itself as defender of the values of the region's media system, arguing that media diversity and freedom of speech is under threat, and they represented unfair competition, as these platform companies pay little tax in the region.

In terms of leadership dimensions, the style of management in this phase was characterized by strong central control and influence, as the ecosystem strategy was attempted implemented from around 2014. While the CEO of Schibsted, Rolv Erik Ryssdal, and the company's board were responsible for this new strategy, Schibsted hired several senior tech executives, amongst others from Google and Twitter, and some of them with McKinsey background, who were given a wide mandate to transform Schibsted through the ecosystem strategy. However, the centralized data-driven ecosystem strategy, and its attempt to operationalize it, lacked sufficient anchoring throughout the company. The long-running issue of centralization and decentralization in decision-making of corporate strategy and its operationalization reached its peak. As such, Schibsted's ecosystem strategy, aiming for a "One company" organization, lay at one end of the central/decentral continuum of corporate strategy decision (Noam, 2019). The implementation of the strategy, and in particular the attempt to create a global online classified advertising platform, did not succeed, as it did not take the company's structure of decentralized power and autonomy into account sufficiently. This again points to the complexities of large international media companies with a decentralized management structure (Doyle, 2013: 37).

96 *Schibsted*

In terms of company dimensions, Schibsted's ambitious ecosystem strategy and its focus on developing a matrix organization across the company along with the overarching "One company" strategic approach proved to be Schibsted at its most centralized. The company's innovation efforts focused on online classified platforms, media platforms, online payment solutions, advertising technology, and data analytics. In terms of corporate culture, such centralization was at odds with Schibsted's corporate culture characterized by short decision-making paths, an emphasis on trust, autonomy, and decentralized company structure. This also showed the power struggle within a company, as despite a hierarchical structure, it proved difficult to locate power within the organization (Deslades, 2016: 313). In fact, in this period, it became even more clear how the editorial culture served as a cushion against centralization and the integration of newspapers. Yet, at the same time, the media and advertising platforms were successfully implemented in both Norway and Sweden, during this period. While Schibsted criticizes the global platform giants, Facebook and Google, its successful launch of media platforms and large market shares in both media and advertising in the region was also criticized, as Schibsted was turning into a regional platform giant.

6 The World's Largest Online Classified Company, the Schibsted Universe, and the Splitting of the Company

2017–2025

The failed attempt to implement the global ecosystem and platform strategy through strong centralization was in stark contrast to the decentralized decision-making within the successful international classified sites and the combination of consolidation yet strong autonomy of the Norwegian and Swedish media houses. The company now had to decide how to move forward in the post-ecosystem strategy period. While in 2017, as much as 71 percent of the company's revenue of NOK 16.9 billion was generated from digital products, underlining the maturity of Schibsted's digital transformation, several major issues were now at stake. Again, the dynamic between centralization and decentralization was at the heart of the situation. The Schibsted group needed to redefine its role in relation to its subsidiaries and brands, after a period of strong centralization. The market and investors continued to put pressure on the company, as the Nordic and international classified businesses were by far the most attractive investment, compared to the media business side. This also proved increasingly challenging for the ownership structure of Schibsted, as Tinius Trust, the largest owner with negative control over the company, had media as its focus. At the same time, Google and Facebook's expansion continued, intensifying competition and transforming the market further. By 2018, the two global giants shared around 25 percent of the total advertising market in Norway. Schibsted and the other news media in the region continued to grapple with how best to compete with them. This chapter details one of the most dramatic periods in the history of Schibsted as the company embarked on dealing with these challenging issues.

Post-Ecosystem Strategies

The issue of how to achieve forms of synergy between the online classified advertising and marketplace business and the media business side had been subject to discussions and corporate strategies since the early 2000s. The issue emerged again in the wake of the abandoned ecosystem strategy: What would

DOI: 10.4324/9781003439431-6

98 *Schibsted*

the benefits of keeping the company together be? Would the opposite be more beneficial? This time the issue was of greater urgency, then previously:

> No doubt our bet on classified sites had been overwhelmingly successful. However, the rapid expansion was a stretch for our financial resources. At the same time our decentralized operational structure and increasingly centralized technology development introduced stress on Schibsted's ability to prioritize and take decisions. This raised a question which we had returned to a couple of times before: What is the ideal company structure? Were the synergies in remaining as one company sufficient? Would the eco system advantages of a united company outweigh the operational stress and capital constraints of staying united?
>
> (Sunde, interview with author, 2024)

By the late 2010s, Schibsted had become a major international company, and creating synergy and collaboration between media and classified had become an even more complex task; Juvik Tveitnes argues:

> Once we had built a global Schibsted, we saw that running a Scandinavian business that is so dominant in its markets, while at the same time maintaining marketplaces in Brazil, was challenging. Where do you actually build the synergies? Schibsted then came to a point where one realized that, in the first instance, we must separate what we call media and what we call marketplaces. The business models are too different. This probably happen in 2017, I think.
>
> (Juvik Tveitnes, interview with author, 2024)

The agendas of these business areas had become very different. Therefore, the company reorganized again. In 2017, Schibsted became organized in Schibsted Media and Schibsted Marketplaces, headed by Raoul Grünthal and Sondre Gravir, respectively. Soon after, in 2018, the company adjusted its organization to Schibsted Media, also headed by Grünthal, and Schibsted Marketplaces International (MPI), at first headed by Gravir. However, Schibsted Media included all Nordic operations – including the Norwegian and Swedish online classified advertising giants, Finn and Blcoket, whereas MPI consisted of all the online classified operations outside of the Nordic region.

This last reorganization was more complicated than perhaps thought of. Two issues were of particular concern. The first was whether the Norwegian classified company, FINN, and the Swedish classified company, Blocket, should be part of the MPI division or the Media division, as these companies would contribute to raising the value of both significantly. It was also a question of whether the strategy of creating synergies between media and classifieds in the two countries was achieving sufficient progress and success. If Blocket and

The World's Largest Online Classified Company 99

FINN had become included in the MPI division, the possibilities for collaboration between the media houses and the classified sites in Norway and Sweden would have ended:

> The profitability of classified far exceeded the margins of our media businesses, even though latter also produced decent returns. This led to a constant pressure from the stock market to split the two divisions. Management was divided on this issue. This disagreement erupted at strategy meeting in Paris in July 2018. In the aftermath of the strategy meeting, the time was ripe to take a decision. Our joint operations in the Nordics gave us a unique reach to digital consumers in a tech savvy and well-off region. My view was that this position would give us a unique advantage both in developing our digital offering and giving us rich data sets advancing our ad sales. The synergies with our international classified sites were weaker and listing them separately would give us the opportunity to promote a further consolidation in the global market.
>
> (Sunde, interview with author, 2024)

Following the Paris meeting in 2018, Schibsted decided that Blocket and FINN should remain within Schibsted's Media division and was not to be included in the international classified MPI division.

A second issue, in relation to the new Schibsted organization, was the position and role of the third business area: Growth and digital venture initiatives. The new Schibsted's Media division included these initiatives in both Sweden and Norway, with a particular focus on the fintech business area. While Schibsted Sweden had long pursued an ecosystem approach, different from the company-wide data-driven ecosystem strategy, in which it invested in and acquired many companies and ventures, utilizing the massive Internet traffic of particularly *Aftonbladet* to promote and market the companies since the 2000s (Barland, 2012, 2013), in Norway the situation was quite different. The Norwegian growth business, Schibsted Vekst (Growth), was formally established in 2010. However, by 2017, the Norwegian side of the growth business could only show to one successful company (Eckblad et al., 2017). Didrik Munch, CEO of Schibsted Norway for nine years, which included the growth and digital venture activity in Norway, until the reorganization of the company in 2017/2018 when he left the company, explains:

> The Swedes were much more into the Growth business. They had much more focus on it, whereas in Norway it seemed more like an ad-hoc thing. We invested a little here and a little there, but we didn't really have it under our skin. I mean Schibsted has been trying to figure this out and working on this the whole time, including myself, when we were working on the Growth part in Norway, and to a certain extent also in Sweden. Because you

100 *Schibsted*

may wonder how much is it connected? How much money are you going to spend on those growth initiatives?

(Munch, interview with author, 2024)

In 2017, the Growth and digital investment initiative was renamed Schibsted Next but remained part of CEO of Schibsted Media, Raoul Grünthal's responsibility until 2021. Grünthal worked to build as strong a position for these initiatives in Norway as in Sweden, but the ecosystem approach developed in Sweden was not easily implemented in Norway. First, you had to get the Norwegian management and the culture bearers to join in. Second, while in Sweden Growth and the other Schibsted businesses had a more equal status in the ecosystem, in Norway FINN and *VG* had dominant positions that extended to the Growth area. Third, at the time, Stockholm was one of the leading hubs for new technology and Internet ventures in Europe, in contrast to Oslo (Grünthal, interview with author, 2024).

The two divisions, Schibsted Media and MPI, continued as planned until September 2018, when Schibsted announced that its classified operations outside the Nordic region was to be spun-off and become an independent listed company, Adevinta. Schibsted consolidated and continued as a Nordic group, headed by its regional media houses and classified marketplaces, along with the growth and venture operations. CEO of Schibsted since 2009, Rolv Erik Ryssdal, the year after, moved into the position of CEO of Adevinta (Schibsted, 2018a). As the new CEO of Schibsted, Kristin Skogen Lund, was appointed on December 1, 2018, a new Schibsted organization was presented, and now the company structure did not include the international marketplaces that was to be spun out the year after. Schibsted implemented a strategy of building a Nordic company consisting of three business areas in three divisions:

Nordic Marketplaces; FINN and asset owner for Blocket (Sweden) and Tori (Finland)
Publishing; will be led by Siv Juvik Tveitnes, previously Head of Publishing operations in the Media Division.
Schibsted Next (Venture investments, Personal Finance, organic growth initiatives incl Distribution); will be led by Raoul Grünthal, previously CEO Schibsted Media. Grünthal will, in addition, have a functional role with the responsibility of boosting growth and entrepreneurship across the company.

(Schibsted, 2018b)

The remaining parts of Schibsted Products and Technology, which had been the organization leading the attempt to implement the earlier ecosystem and platform strategy, was split between the international classified division, and the remaining Nordic marketplaces and media divisions (Eckblad, 2018). Still, while Schibsted emphasized having moved away from the ambition to centralize as with its earlier ecosystem strategy, the company did not abandon the idea

The World's Largest Online Classified Company   101

of the Schibsted group playing an important role across the company and its individual subsidiaries and brands.

The Schibsted Pyramid

In 2018, the key task for the new CEO of Schibsted, Kristin Skogen Lund, was to reestablish the new Schibsted, without the international classified business, which was to be spun out as Adevinta. The way Skogen Lund decided to organize the new Schibsted was very much tied to her view on the dynamic between centralization and decentralization within the company. In contrast to the earlier ecosystem and platform strategy and the idea of a matrix organization across the company, Skogen Lund argued that Schibsted should not aim for further centralization. Instead, Schibsted centrally should position itself in a more supportive role of its individual subsidaries, companies and brands. A Schibsted organizational pyramid was organized with the corporate aim of "Empowering people" at the top, with all the Schibsted-owned companies in the middle, and the Schibsted group as a foundation at the bottom:

> The pyramid was established because I did not want Schibsted to be seen as something that stood above the companies. I wanted everyone to think of Schibsted as a platform that everyone could lean on, and a foundation they stood on. It has been quite successful, rhetorically and conceptually, because the Schibsted companies have always had very strong autonomy with employees who have very little faith in authority. It was therefore important to ensure that the Schibsted group was something that contributed and made the companies stronger. Not something at the top that was to determine and limit. The strong autonomy is much of the reason for the success, because there is a lot of innovative power in this "anarchy." Anarchy is a bit of a strong word, but there is something unruly about the Schibsted culture.
>
> (Skogen Lund, interview with author, 2024)

Schibsted centrally took charge of company-wide initiatives that demanded scale, for example large technology investments, and platform development, but also investment and recruitment of specialized competence, for example, within data privacy that the individual companies not necessarily had. The company's data strategy represented such a key initiative from Schibsted centrally:

> One of the most important things, after I began as CEO in 2018, was that with GDPR, we could no longer share data. Before, *Aftenposten* owned its data, and *VG* owned its data and FiNN owned its data. Whereas today it is Schibsted that owns all data, so you log in to Schibsted, and we can register data regardless of which service you are on, and this also means that we

102 *Schibsted*

have a much richer data profile on you than we would otherwise have in a silo structure per company. And it's a tremendous value because everything we do is so data-driven, so it's perhaps the best example of an ecosystem.

(Skogen Lund, interview with author, 2024)

This contributed to Schibsted's focus on collecting first-party data, generated through its data strategy. A challenge for particularly smaller online newspapers' ability to make use of user data is that to utilize such data one needs enormous amounts of first-party data. Most single newspaper sites do not have the necessary Internet traffic to generate such amounts of data nor the competence to utilize such data. One solution is for a local newspaper to be acquired by a larger news organization to get access to such technology and connect with the digital economy (Sjovaag, 2019). Another solution has been collaboration between smaller newspapers. In the United States, 5,000 local newspapers have agreed to share data in a digital advertising system, through The Local News Consortium (Lindblad, 2021).

In the face of competition from the global platforms, Schibsted has argued for more collaboration between news media companies in Norway, particuarly to be able to collect large amounts of user data to enable accurate, personalized advertising and media content targeted to users (Ryssdal, 2016). The Schibsted universe, into which all subscribers logged on to, aimed to ensure sufficient access to first-party data, and thereby provide an alternative platform for advertisers and media content distribution and consumption. By 2021, Schibsted had 3 million daily logged in users in Norway and Sweden.

Nordic Marketplaces – Verticalization

In 2021, the idea of creating a Nordic marketplace platform began to take form to meet increased competition from both local and international services expanding into region. Schibsted's Nordic marketplaces have historically had strongest position in Norway and Sweden, through particularly FINN and Blocket, but in recent years expanded in Finland and Denmark. In 2020, the Okotie online marketplace was acquired from the Finnish media giant, Sanoma, for around NOK 2 billion. Having lauched the number one general Finish marketplace, Tori, in 2009, the acquisition of Okiotie, with the number one position in jobs and major position in real estate, marked Schibsted's ambitious expansion in Finland (Schibsted, 2020). The acquisition of eBay's classified operations, in 2021, which also included stand-alone online marketplaces, DBA.dk, the leading general online marketplace in Denmark, and bilbasen.dk, online marketplace for trading cars, marked Schibsted's intention of becoming the leading player in Denmark (Schibsted, 2021b).

In 2021, the Schibsted Next division was split, as Distribution and E-commerce became part of the Nordic marketplace operation, and a new

Growth division was established, and titled Financial Services and Ventures, with the remaining companies and investments from Schibsted Next (Jerijervi, 2021). This development can be traced back to when Christian Printzell Halvorsen returned to Schibsted, in 2019, and became SVP of Nordic marketplaces. The focus was now on turning the marketplaces from being only an advertising platform into services that supported "the consumer's entire customer journey," so called "going transactional" with integrated payment, insurance, and shipping. The plan to create a Nordic marketplace platform was launched formally in 2021, under the project name, Sunstone, and in early 2022, a further reorganization began and was in place in early 2023. Christian Printzell Halvorsen, the current CEO of Schibsted Marketplaces, but at the time EVP of Nordic marketplaces, e-commerce, and distribution, explains:

> We simply merged our organizations across the Nordics into one large organization. Instead of organizing ourselves around FINN and Blocket and so on, we organized around recommerce, mobility, real estate and jobs, across the Nordic region. It wasn't a centralization, but the intention was something of the same, namely that you create larger units with more scale., But we had learned a little from the experiences we made in the "One Company" era, where we saw that it easily creates friction between the local and the central. Instead of thinking local-central, everyone is in a unit, in a way.
> (Printzell Halvorsen, interview with author, 2024)

The online marketplace companies in the four Nordic countries were now organized in the four verticals: recommerce, mobility, real estate, and jobs. The aim was to increase competitiveness, make more efficient investments, and share technology solutions across the national marketplaces, to achieve economies of scale. Still, the user continued to access the new organization through the national marketplace brands.

Nordic Media Houses – Subscriptions, User Payment, and Content Marketing

The Norwegian and Swedish media houses were successful in establishing digital platforms for both publishing and advertising, from the mid-2010s onward. In 2018, Schibsted began to focus on developing the "Schibsted universe" into which users log in to consume Schibsted's media and services, which generated user data and aimed to enable the targeting of the users with advertising, services, and media products. Through its data strategy, the company's media houses have increasingly attempted to become more "user centric" and improve the "user experience" for the individual media users, but similarly to the company's online marketplaces, the media users "transaction journey" is also important; former CEO of Schibsted, Kristin Skogen Lund, explains: "The

104 *Schibsted*

biggest problem with Google and Facebook is that they have taken the advertising revenue, not all of it, but a large share. And, then we made two main moves: subscriptions and user payment, and new advertising concepts" (Skogen Lund, interview with author, 2024).

News Subscriptions and User Payment

While advertising revenue was the most important source of income for the newspapers in Norway before 2015, since then income from user payment has become their main source of income (Medietilsynet, 2023), so is the case with Schibsted. From having the vast majority of income from advertising, the situation has become the opposite, as the majority of income comes from user payment.

By 2023, user payment made up 62.8 percent of the total revenues of newspapers in Norway, and 33.3 percent from advertising. This is a radical change from 2013, when 51.3 percent of revenues were generated from advertising, and 44.2 percent from user payment (Medietilsynet, 2024: 12). Internationally, Norway and Sweden, have the highest proportion of users paying for news (Newman et al., 2024: 11). By 2016, Schibsted's news media surpassed 510,000 digital subscribers in Norway and Sweden. In 2020, the number of subscribers had increased to 800,000 digital subscribers and in total 1.3 million including print and other subscriptions. Then in 2021, the number of digital subscriptions reached 1,000,000 and 1.5 million in total. Still, to maintain the growth in user payment and subscription, news companies see the need to continually develop and market their offerings. In recent years, the *New York Times* and Schibsted, along with public broadcasters, are among the large publishers who have expanded into the podcast format to also compete with Spotify (Newman et al., 2024: 31). *PodMe*, Schibsted's major podcast platform, was launched in 2017 in Sweden, and by 2021 Schibsted had a 91 percent ownership, offering subscription-based podcasts from both its media houses and independent producers in Norway, Sweden, and Finland. By 2021, the service had over 100.000 subscribers (Schibsted, 2021a).

Since 2020, the offering of bundle subscriptions that gives access across the company's different media brands has become a wider trend and common way of packaging and combining editorial content for the large news companies (Medietilsynet, 2023: 30). Launched in 2020, the Norwegian news company, Amedia's +Alt subscription gives access to over 100 newspapers, podcasts, and video offerings (Medietilsynet, 2023: 10). In 2022, Schibsted launched the "Full access" online subscription, giving access to all media content for Norwegian users from the newspapers *Aftenposten*, *VG*, *Bergens Tidende*, *Stavanger Aftenblad*, E24, to the podcast platform *PodMe* and over 50 magazines (Schibsted, 2022c). The "Full access" media subscription represented a similar development to Schibsted's Nordic marketplace verticals and platforms that

The World's Largest Online Classified Company 105

cut across brands and give access to the whole Schibsted universe of media content:

> Those who have that type of subscription, they become much more loyal, first of all, and then they use us much more, and it doesn't cost us anything that you read *Aftenposten* online. It does not increase any marginal costs. On the contrary, we get the more data from you. So, we become even better at serving you as a customer, because we get even more of this data currency that is so important. The brands are very important, but you cannot limit yourself to silos, because then you also limit your potential too much.
>
> (Skogen Lund, interview with author, 2024)

The next step in the development of such bundle subscriptions is a more personal, user-targeted subscription. Since 2023, Amedia has offered through its +Alt service a personally tailored news stream with editorial content from their newspapers that users had shown a particular interest in (Medietilsynet, 2023: 34). On the one hand, the trend of offering bundle subscription represents an opportunity for smaller newspapers outside of the large news companies. They may become partners in, for example, +Alt, and thereby get access to income, technology, and infrastructure. It could be a way of securing the economic sustainability of smaller newspapers and could thereby contribute to maintaining a certain media diversity in ownership, as a counterweight to the increasing consolidation in the newspaper sector (Medietilsynet, 2023: 34). The Norwegian news company, Amedia's bundle subscription Alt+, and Schibsted's Full Tillgang are attracting 10 percent and 6 percent of subscribers, respectively (Newman et al., 2024). On the other hand, this again exemplifies how the largest news media companies and structures continue to be able to exploit and benefit from the logic of the digital market. In the Nordic region, the newspapers and news media companies that are part of large media groups are the most successful, benefiting from economies of scale, and Schibsted is one of them (Lindberg, 2023: 89).

Content Marketing and Advertising Technology

The second initiative to increase revenue was through utilizing advertising technology and user data to develop new advertising concepts. One such concept is content marketing, popular among many large Scandinavian media companies, where content is produced to promote products and services, which have the looks of journalistic content (Sjovaag, 2023: 88), *VG*'s *Partnerstudio* was launched already in 2015, and later the company-wide Schibsted Partnerstudio, serving all of Schibsted's Norwegian newspapers was formed, Skogen Lund elaborates:

> We are very successful with new advertising concepts, for example, content marketing. What you typically see on *VG*, and which is marked as an

advertisement, but there is in a way a content in it. It sells very well, so we have managed to innovate in terms of formats. Google and Facebook cannot convey that type of advertisement to the same extent.

(Skogen Lund, interview with author, 2024)

In fact, Schibsted claims that the click rates of content marketing or branded content outperform display advertising, and the time spent on such content is comparable with editorial content (Schibsted, 2023b). However, the content marketing phenomena has been criticized as many fear that it undermines the credibility of journalism. The controversy has subsided and there seems to be a general acceptance of content marketing as representing a significant income for news organizations (Sjovaag, 2019: 88). An important point is how advertisers are more conscious about the context their advertisements appear, and the Schibsted universe may be considered a safer place to advertise than other parts of the online landscape (Skogen Lund, interview with author, 2024).

Adevinta – the World's Largest Online Classified Advertising Company

The portfolio of international online classified companies was not part of the new Schibsted, CEO Kristin Skogen Lund announced in 2018. Instead, Marketplace International, was spun out and stock-listed. It was the largest stock listing since the listing of the former Norwegian public telecom company, Telenor. The remaining parts of Schibsted were split into three divisions: Nordic Marketplaces, News Media, and Next, as previously outlined (Schibsted, 2022a).

While Schibsted's international classified operations consisted of 46 sites in around 30 countries in 2014, a process of consolidating and divesting its classified portfolio took place from then on with the aim to include the most financially attractive and with the strongest market positions in the portfolio of Adevinta. At the time of the listing, Adevinta, with 2,800 employees, consisted of online classified services in 16 countries. These included France, Spain, Italy, Austria, Ireland, Hungary, the joint venture in Brazil, and companies in an earlier, investment phase in Mexico, Chile, Belarus, Colombia, Dominican Republic, Morocco, and Tunisia, and the mobile service, Shpock, in the United Kingdom (Adevinta, 2018).

The most important motives for spinning out Adevinta were financial gain and the ability to navigate the market more independently than when the international online classified business was part of the Schibsted company structure. Schibsted and its largest shareholder, the Tinius Trust, through its holding company Blommenholm Industries AS, were to initially have as much as 59.3 percent and 7.8 percent ownership share, respectively. This represented major financial holdings as Adevinta was valued at NOK 53 billion when listed. While Schibsted's portfolio of international online classified companies had been restricted by the governance structure, dominated by the Tinius Trust,

The World's Largest Online Classified Company 107

which was not to reduce its size of shareholdings, this was not the case with the independent Adevinta. Aleksander Rosinski, advisor of Schibsted's investment in Adevinta for several years and former board member of Adevinta, elaborates:

> It was important that Adevinta was a company that did not have the governance restrictions that Schibsted's international classified advertising business had adhered to. The company needed to be able to develop and buy other companies with shares, among other things.
>
> (Rosinski, interview with author, 2023)

Without such governance restrictions, Adevinta was able to make the biggest international acquisition in Norway's financial history, buying eBay's Classified Group for USD 9.2 billion. Schibsted acquired online classified sites in 20 markets, turning Adevinta into the "World's largest online classified company," being the market leader in 16 countries (eBay, 2020; Adevinta, 2021). As such, the spin out of Adevinta created several financial benefits and corporate advantages, according to the first CEO of Adevinta, Rolv Erik Ryssdal (2019–2022) and this made the acquisition of the eBay Classified Group possible. There were three bidders for eBay's classified division, but Schibsted succeeded:

> There were some advantages in creating Adevinta. Investors will be able to deal with a company that could have full focus and power on classifieds and be a more attractive partner. What turned out, when we bought eBay classifieds, was precisely that we were an attractive alliance partner who could pay with shares. It was a deal of around NOK 90 billion, but around 2/3 of the settlement was us giving (Adevinta) shares to them. After all, they had never accepted shares in a company that ran Norwegian newspapers. It enabled new structures in a completely different way. Adevinta became a pure play company, and that created a good number of other opportunities, and it proved to be of crucial importance for us to be able to do the large deal with eBay.
>
> (Ryssdal, interview with author, 2024)

Through Adevinta, investors could finally invest in a pure play international classified advertising company without having to take Schibsted's, from an investor's perspective, financially far less attractive news media division as part of the deal. The eBay deal showed exactly how Adevinta, independently listed and without the governance restrictions of Schibsted and the Tinius Trust, became a much more powerful and attractive corporate partner as it could sell and issue new stocks to pay for acquisitions. Schibsted paid eBay a total of USD 2.5 billion in cash and 540 million shares of Adevinta. This gave eBay a 44 percent owner share in Adevinta, which were to be reduced to no more than 33 percent, and Schibsted retained around 33percent (eBay, 2020; Adevinta, 2021).

108 *Schibsted*

The Split of Schibsted's Nordic Media and Marketplaces Businesses

Then in late 2023, perhaps the most dramatic decision in Schibsted's history was announced: the decision to split the company. This came as a surprise to many, after a seemingly calmer period following the ambitious, but failed attempt to develop a global online classfied advertising platform and ecosystem strategy. In 2018, the Schibsted group centrally was positioned in a more supporting role and as a foundation for its subsidiaries and brands. Schibsted's international marketplace division, Adevinta, had been spun out, with Schibsted as the major shareholder, and following eBay Classified acquisition turned Adevinta into the world's largest classified advertising company. Acquisitions of marketplaces in Denmark and Finland marked the development of a Nordic marketplace giant.

The dramatic events leading up to the split were in particular triggered and set in motion by the significant drop in the company's A stock value from over NOK 450 in late 2021 to just over NOK 150 in June 2022. The company needed to act to show resolve and create clarity, not least to regain the confidence of the market, yet how and in which strategic direction to move, was not evident. The issue of Schibsted's strategic priority and the question as to why investors should invest in Schibsted, came up again. As so often throughout much of Schibsted's digital transformation and internationalization, the divergence between media and online classifieds came to the fore: investors viewed marketplaces as the financial attraction, in contrast to media that, from an investor's perspective, did not justify investments to the same extent as it generated far less profits and had less potential. At the same time, Chairman of Schibsted Ole Jacob Sunde retired from his position he had held for over 20 years, and board member for many years, Karl Christian Agerup, also a former McKinsey consultant, took over the position on 4 May, 2022. Schibsted's stock value reached a low in June, and now had to show decisiveness and resoluteness but was not sure how to move forward. In the autumn of 2022, the Sigma project, promoted by the Tinius Trust, Schibsted's largest and controlling owner, suggested a strategic direction involving a far deeper integration and a more seamless organization of Schibsted and its brands and subsidiaries in a system resembling the major integrated, more product-focused, and cloud-based companies, such as Google.

Parallel to these events, a consortium of global private equity investors, Primera and Blackstone, had been interested for a long time in buying Adevinta and privatize and de-list the company. Schibsted, with major ownership in Adevinta, and the Tinius Trust would benefit immensely financially from such a deal. In the summer of 2023, the Sigma project's suggested strategic direction was rejected by the Schibsted board. Then, in early autumn 2023, as the Adevinta deal was close to being completed, the Tinus Trust turned around and offered to buy all Schibsted's media assets. The offer was accepted by the company. Soon after, the Adevinta deal was officially announced in November. Schibsted and the Tinius Trust was to receive NOK billions from the sale of parts of their ownership in Adevinta. This transaction enabled the Tinius Trust financially to make the offer of aquiring all Schibsted's news media assets, which was announced in December 2023. The formal split up of Schibsted took place in May 2024.

While the story of Schibsted's digital transformation and international expansion is the story of numerous reorganizations, mergers and acquisitions, and divestments, the split of the company represented a far more fundamental change.

The Three Deals Shaping the Split and Future of Schibsted

There were three key deals of particular relevance for the split of Schibsted and the way the different parts were organized. In late 2023, Schibsted announced two major transactions, which were to change the company fundamentally and structurally.

First, on November 21, 2023, after around two years of working on this deal, the global financial giants Permira and Blackstone offered, with funds advised by them, to acquire 60 percent of Schibsted's 28.1 percent ownership in Adevitna for NOK 24 billion, of which NOK 20 billion was to be paid as dividend to the Schibsted shareholders, of which the Tinius Trust, the largest shareholder, would be the main beneficiary. Schibsted announced it would accept the offer, and its remaining stake in Adevinta would now be 13.6 percent. The value of the Adevinta share offered to the Adevinta shareholders was set at NOK 115 and corresponded to a total value of Adevinta of around NOK 141 billion, and Schibsted's ownership stake valued at around NOK 40 billion (Schibsted, 2023c).

Second, on December 11, 2023, Schibsted announced the splitting of the company: separating the company into Schibsted Media and Schibsted Marketplaces. Schibsted and Tinius Trust, until now the largest shareholder and with negative control, agreed for the Trust to acquire the company's News Media business area, its ownership share in the Norwegian news company, Polaris Media, as well as other media holdings. The Tinius Trust paid a total of NOK 6.2 billion, of which NOK 5.4 billion for Schibsted's News Media business, and NOK 0.8 billion for the shares in the media group, Polaris Media. The deal included the key Norwegian news media brands and companies *VG* and *Aftenposten* and the regional media houses, and *Aftonbladet* and *Svenska Dagbladet*, in Sweden. In addition, digital niche products such as the podcast company, *Podme*, the online financial news site, *E24, Shifter*, and *Fri Flyt*, was part of the deal. The deal also include ownership in media companies NTB, TT Nyhetsbyrån, Retriever, and Lokalavisene (Schibsted, 2023d, 2024a).

A third transaction in early 2024 was Schibsted's decision to acquire Polaris Media's 9.99 percent share in the Norwegian classified company FINN and take full control of the company. The transaction also showed the

110   *Schibsted*

immense increase in the value of the FINN company. Per Axel Koch, CEO of Polaris Media, pointed out that: "This brings our initial investment in 2000 of NOK 5 million in FINN to a new level whereby our shares are exchanged for shares in Schibsted for a total consideration of NOK 2.5 billion" (Schibsted, 2024b).

Schibsted's remaining stock-listed company, named Schibsted Marketplaces, headed by the new CEO, Christian Printzell Halvorsen, also a former McKinsey consultant, consisted of the fully owned Nordic marketplaces: FINN (Norway), Blocket (Sweden), Tori (Finland), DBA (Denmark), Okiote (Finland) and Bilbasen, and the Delivery operations, as well as the Growth and Investments, which mainly included the fintech companies, Lendo, Prisjakt, MittAnbud (Schibsted, 2024c, 2024d).

Together the three deals showed the enormous difference in the financial value of Schibsted's media businesses and the online classified and marketplace operations. While the former was valued at NOK 6.2 billion, the FINN deal showed how this company alone was valued at around NOK 25 billion, and the international online classified advertising operations Schibsted had developed and spun out as Adevinta was valued at around NOK 141 billion.

Why the Split?

At a fundamental level, the split was about the key corporate dynamics that has characterized the decision-making and strategies throughout the digital transformation and internationalization of Schibsted: between, on the one hand, forms of centralization, synergies, and coordination and, on the other hand, forms of decentralization, independence, and autonomy, along with the external market conditions.

When Schibsted announced the split in 2023, the company argued that the rationale for the separation between the news media and Nordic marketplace divisions (including the Financial Services and Ventures) was mainly two things:

> [T]he continued verticalization of Nordic Marketplaces is hard to combine with the vision of creating a more integrated Schibsted for the next few years, and News Media's long-term strategy requires investments that often compete with the financially more attractive opportunities related to our marketplaces.
>
> (Schibsted, 2023d)

Schibsted was engaged in several parallel, resource demanding processes through the Sunstone project's verticalization of its Nordic marketplaces, and the ongoing need for investments in media, and the costs of keeping the company together, that were deemed high. Ole Jacob Sunde emphasizes the

The World's Largest Online Classified Company 111

strategic shift in the wake of the Adevinta spin-off, focusing on the Nordic region, as one reason for the split:

> Since the split in 2018 and the IPO of Adevinta in 2019, the Schibsted strategy was set on building a Nordic, digital growth company. During 2022/23 it became clear that these efforts did not yield the desired results. One obstacle was a major and well-designed verticalization of the classified sites, moving from a geographical to a product led organization. The individual vertical would run across several geographies based on the same technology stack. On the media side, this change had been executed already, as editorial systems and ad platforms were common for all our titles in Norway and Sweden. The board was also struggling with the capital allocation. The media business needed continued investments however could not match the returns of the classified sites.
>
> (Sunde, interview with author, 2024)

Thoroughout the digital and international expansion, the media businesss had increasingly been viewed very differently by investors and the stock market, and the biggest owner, Tinius Trust. The latter having media as its core focus, as stated in its Articles of Association. While Schibsted has had to invest in media, this has not been received well by the stock market (Printzell Halvorsen, interview with author, 2024). One example of how sensitive the market is to media investments is exemplified by Schibsted's much criticized acquisition of 10 percent of the international audiovisual streaming service, Viaplay:

> We invested NOK 300 (340) million in Viaplay, and then the share price plummeted by a total of around NOK 6 billion. It was a very clear sign that the stock market does not want us to invest in media. I know you can always argue that there was no faith in Viaplay itself, but I think a large part of the effect was an anxiety that we should now start putting much more money into media. It became very clear and exemplified by the reaction to the Viaplay investment.
>
> (Skogen Lund, interview with author, 2024)

The split has also to do with lack of strategic clarity. Raoul Grünthal, appointed CEO of Schibsted Sweden in 2009 and CEO of Schibsted Next (Growth) from 2018 to 2021, and thereby one of the key proponents of the company's growth and venture initiatives, argues that the Growth ecosystem culture, which had been strong in Sweden, was difficult to maintain and foster:

> It was a culture and a strategy that was quite difficult for an outsider to understand, it was so different. I saw it as my mission to ensure that it survived when the Adevinta structure disappeared, and the new Nordic

112 *Schibsted*

Schibsted emerged. But in practice it became difficult, the new strategy was neither black nor white, it ended up somewhere between product and ecosystem.

(Grünthal, interview with author, 2024)

In fact, former CEO Kristin Skogen Lund argue that the market forces have had a major impact on the company as they are pulling in the direction of specialization and not integration:

Where you used to depend on the marketplaces getting help from large digital distribution from the media, these are now so strong in their own right that they need each other less. That is the fundamental thing here, just to be clear. The value of splitting the company is much greater than what you can gain from closer integration, and especially when it was difficult to find a clear recipe for success for something that has not been tried before.

(Skogen Lund, interview with author, 2024)

The discussions on keeping Schibsted together has been a recurring discussion, as some have favored keeping the Nordic media and marketplaces together, while others argued for splitting them. The Tinus Trust's wish to keep these business areas together became particularly evident during the discussions in Paris in 2018. In 2022/2023, the Tinius Trust again wished to explore this strategy of integrating the company further, through the Sigma project, but instead ended up buying Schibsted media division and holdings. Kristin Skogen Lund, former CEO of Schibsted, sees parallels between the major ecosystem strategy (2014–2017) and the Sigma project initiative (2022–2023),

The London project was strategically well thought out. I have often thought that if we had succeeded in creating a common platform for the whole of Schibsted and Adevinta, it would have been a formidable strength, and I really wish we had achieved that. But it was unfortunately the case that it was a strategically ambitious idea that one was not able to execute well. Both (Ecosystem and Sigma) are examples of that. There was resistance both times. What happened the first time, I wasn't there then, but I've heard a lot about it, was that the initiative was centralized in London and then lost a bit of ground contact in relation to the rest of the organization. Schibsted was highly decentralized, not least represented by Antoine Jouteau who managed (Lecoinboin) in France, which was the largest classified unit. It was not possible to get "buy-in" from him and from the important, locally run businesses that offered resistance, so that it became completely impossible to achieve it. It was somewhat similar with Sigma, but it was far from as dramatic and expensive. But it was probably a bit the same; top-down ideology that harmonizes rather poorly with the cultural reality of the company.

(Skogen Lund, interview with author, 2024)

The World's Largest Online Classified Company 113

In contrast to Schibsted's major ecosystem strategy and its matrix organization the Sigma initiative and idea was never attempted realized. However, both aimed for a strategic direction of a deeper integrated and more seamless organization of the Schibsted brands and subsidiaries. These approaches represented top-down centralization initiatives that may be appealing and attractive ideas and make sense in theory, but are difficult to implement successfully in such a decentralized company but also because market forces pull in the opposite direction, in this case. The fact that Schibsted was engaged in the costly Sunstone project, and the media business-side in ongoing need for investments, not least in terms of technology, along with the history of trying to integrate the company's parts and businesses to create synergies, contributed to making the highly ambitious idea of the Sigma project less realistic.

While the division of Schibsted meant that the company's data ecosystem or universe was split with different logins for Schibsted Marketplaces and Schibsted Media, the launch of the bundle subscription giving access to all media content and the establishment of a Nordic online marketplace company through verticalization and by "going transactional" reflect forms of closer integration, but within each of the two business areas.

The New Schibsted Marketplaces Company

After the split of Schibsted in 2024, the remaining stock-listed company, Schibsted Marketplaces, with around 1,500 employees, consisted of the Nordic online marketplaces and the growth and investment assets. It aimed to become an integrated Nordic marketplace company comprising of national marketplace brands such as FINN (Norway), Blocket (Sweden), Tori (Finland), DBA (Denmark), Oikotie (Finland), and Bilbasen, but also Delivery and distribution operations in Norway, along with the Growth and Investments portfolio of particularly fintech companies such as Lendo, Prisjakt, and MittAnbud and venture companies and investments in an early stage phase (Schibsted, 2024d).

Despite using the national brands such as FINN and Blocket, through a strategy of verticalization, the marketplace business is organized in four verticals: mobility, recommerce, real estate, and jobs, instead of countries. The aim is now to create common platforms and focus investments in the four verticals across four countries. At the same time, Schibsted Marketplaces represented a move away from just being an advertisement platform to becoming increasingly "transactional," by taking positions in the whole value chain of the marketplace transactions, which requires major investments (Schibsted, 2024d).

However, soon after the formation of the new Schibsted Marketplace company, the company announced a further streamlining and strengthened focus on the marketplace operations as businesses not considered as core for the new company were to be divested. Its main fintech company, the Lendo Group, established in Sweden in 2007, along with Prisjakt, the skilled trades marketplaces and jobs marketplaces in Sweden and Finland, focusing on Norway, as

114 *Schibsted*

well as the main part of its portfolio of venture investments, was to be sold (Schibsted, 2024e). However, this also marked the end of Schibsted's focus on digital growth and venture initiatives, dating back to *Aftonbladet*'s establishment of Tilväxtmedier in 2006 and on a group level, Schibsted Tilväxtmedier formed in 2009 in Sweden and later expanding in Norway.

The New Schibsted Media Company

The now Tinius Trust-owned Schibsted Media's ambition is to be "the leading media destination in the Nordic region," according to its CEO Siv Juvik Tveitnes (Juvik Tveitnes quoted in Schibsted Media, 2024). The company, formed in 2024 with over 2,500 employees, first consisted of mainly the media houses *Aftonbladet* and *Svenska Dagbladet* in Sweden and *Aftenposten* and *VG*, along with the regional media houses, in Norway. Since the mid-2010s, the news media side of Schibsted has developed and succeeded in creating publishing and advertising platforms across these news companies. The news companies have clearly achieved and benefited from scale and synergies in several ways and will not be hurt by the split of Schibsted; Ole Jacob Sunde, argues:

> From the Tinius Trust perspective, we saw that a separation and specialization of the two units had merit, despite dyssynergies in advertising and common enterprise technology. Over time a split would reduce complexities and cost and allow the two businesses to excel in market areas which were developing in different directions. The Trust had grown from a modest beginning to hold substantial capital and could become a credible owner of the media assets. The purpose would be unchanged, producing quality journalism, which was financially sustainable, but the trust could take a longer view and require a lower financial return than a listed company.
>
> (Sunde, interview with author, 2024)

In fact, Tinius Trust's acquisition reflects the wider trend in recent years of foundations and trusts as the most proactive in acquiring newspapers and news companies in the region (Sjovaag, 2023). By, 2025, six of the ten largest newsmedia companies in the Nordic region are owned by foundations or trusts, and two of the top ten companies that are stock-listed had foundations or trusts as the largest single shareholder (Lindberg, 2023: 34–35). While Tinius Trust's acquisition has been very positively received, former CEO of Schibsted, Kristin Skogen Lund, central in making the take-over happen, also points to more critical aspects in relation to the establishment of the new Schibsted Media company.

> The media will not have to deal with the stock exchange, but they will have to be profitable, and it is not a given that they will be allowed to invest that much more. There are probably some illusions here that can be broken. The Tinius Trust may become risk averse with so many eggs in one basket. A lot had to go wrong in Schibsted before Schibsted would go down, with

The World's Largest Online Classified Company 115

the enormous power in the marketplace business. Pure media ownership is more vulnerable. Finally, the division implies a sharp concentration of media power in a very few hands. It becomes important to manage it wisely.

(Skogen Lund, interview with author, 2024)

In fact, already in late 2024, this new reality began to dawn on Schibsted Media's media houses. The company announced NOK 500 million in cost reductions, due to the levelling out of revenues from digital advertising and subscriptions, cutting 350 man-years, a total of 13 percent of its workforce, with the aim of making the company profitable in 2025. In response, the representatives of the editorial staff of all the Schibsted-owned Norwegian media houses expressed disappointment and demanded the owner, the Tinius Trust, to take a more active role and instead invest parts of its large capital base on development and innovation in key, capital-intensive areas such as audio and audiovisual products and services (Fossen et al., 2024; Solgård, 2025). Video is key to increasing monetization of sports, live events, and entertainment. Another key area of innovation for Schibsted Media is artificial intelligence. While Schibsted Media's newsrooms have adopted AI in some form, these are mainly applied to current and existing tasks such as news gathering, workflows, and the versioning of content to different audiences and formats. Schibsted Media's pioneering partnership with OpenAI, is arguably the company's most adventurous, but also criticised, AI move to date. Editorial content is incorporated in the latter's services, including ChatGPT, while the former gets insights and access to technology. However, Schibsted has yet to make more substantial changes or bets to meet the possible fundamental changes in the structure of news, although work to map out different AI scenarios (Schibsted Media, 2025a).

It is important for the new Schibsted Media company to be innovative and risk-taking, former CEO of Schibsted Sweden, Raoul Grünthal, argues. A challenge for the new Schibsted Media is to avoid becoming too similar to other news companies: "Schibsted has developed and evolved not through protectionism or by being nostalgic, but by being daring and taking risks in its often-challenging digital transformation" (Grünthal, interview with author, 2024). Similarly, Rolv Erik Ryssdal, former CEO of Schibsted (2009–2018), emphasizes that while the Tinius Trust will provide long-term security, it is important that the news media houses continue to be proactive and innovative: "It is important that newspapers are not considered a sunset industry, not least in terms of attracting competent people. They must somehow be a vibrating system that is constantly developing" (Ryssdal, interview with author, 2024). There is a need to find a new balance between the new Schibsted Media company and the individual news media houses in terms of centralization and decentralization of decision-making to remain agile, Gard Steiro, Chief Editor and CEO of *VG*, points out (Steiro, interview with author, 2023).

One continuing key trend in the Nordic region, with particular relevance for the issue of centralization and decentralization, is the further acquisitions, consolidation and joint efforts among the large news and media companies

116 *Schibsted*

(Lindberg, 2023). Throughout the 2020s, Schibsted's relation with Polaris Media, Norway's third largest news media company, in which the new Schibsted Media holds around a 30 percent ownership, is one of its key strategic developments. This relation stretches back to the second half of the 1990s when the now Polaris Media owned newspaper, *Adresseavisen*, collaborated in advertising with Schibsted's then co-owned regional newspapers. In 2024, two of Schibsted's major Nordic news media competitors made major strategic moves. The Norwegian Ameida acquired the Danish news company, Berlingske, and the Swedish Bonnier News Media and NWT Media, the latter holding an around 27 percent owner share in Polaris Media, entered a partnership (Waatland, 2024). Then, in 2025, Schibsted Media announced the acquisition of Telia Company's TV & Media business for SEK 6.55 billion. This included TV4 in Sweden and MTV in Finland, two of the most popular television and media brands in these countries and described as "national cornerstone" institutions in terms of news and media content (Schibsted Media, 2025b). This marked the resurrection of Schibsted's earlier ambition of creating a Nordic television company. In the mid-2000s, Schibsted failed in its attempt to acquire TV4 and the Finnish media company, Alma Media, and decided to sell its stake in TV4 and TV2 Norway. Now, the newly formed Schibsted Media's ambition of becoming a Nordic leading media company proved to also include a major expansion in television.

The characteristics of the Nordic media system and market are fundamental for the expansion, position, and role of these large news media companies in these societies. Traditionally, the region's population has been the world's most avid news consumers. The willingness to pay for news is among the highest and so is the level of freedom of speech and press freedom in these countries. The early roll-out of broadband and rapid take-up of smartphones across the region reflects the focus on technology as key to develop these societies and the fast adoption of new technologies. CEO of Schibsted New Media argues: "There is something about our entire society and the entire infrastructure and digital maturity that helps us" (Juvik Tveitnes, interview with author, 2024).

Furthermore, news outlets in the Nordic region stand out internationally as the main source for news, compared to social media and search engines. As much as 59 percent in Norway and 51 percent in Sweden access news directly at news publishers online. While in Norway as little as 10 percent accesses news through social media and 23 percent through online search and aggregator portals, and in Sweden 12 percent uses social media for news and 21 percent uses for search and aggregators (Newman et al., 2024: 21). Schibsted's largest newspapers, *Aftonbladet*, in Sweden, and *VG*, in Norway, are primary news destinations: "They are the biggest sites in each country by far, and that is because they were early to digitize, and have been digitized before the global platforms came along" (Juvik Tveitnes, interview with author, 2024).

While platforms including Facebook, Google, X – formerly Twitter, and TikTok are becoming a more important source and destination for information and news, there are clearly differences between countries and their news media systems. These differences, at least to some extent, are explained by

The World's Largest Online Classified Company   117

"path dependency," as "historic strength of the printed newspaper industry is highly correlated with the extent to which people today tend to rely on direct access to news websites and apps rather than accessing news via social media platforms" (Nielsen and Fletcher, 2023: 486).

The strong direct connection and contact between news publishers and readers is also reflected in the willingness to pay for news. In Norway, 40 percent paid for news the last year, while the average for 20 international markets is 17 percent. In Sweden, 31 percent pays for online news in the last year, compared to around 22 percent in the United States, while only 13 percent and 11 percent in Germany and France (Newman et al., 2024: 22, 55). Still, there are challenges. The global phenomena of fake news and disinformation may undermine trust in information and news and journalism. Internationally, the number of respondents "who are worried about what is real and what is fake on the internet overall is up" from 56 to 59 percent, according to the Reuters Digital News Report 2024. The highest level of concern is found in Africa (81 percent), the United States (72 percent), and the United Kingdom (70 percent), the lowest is in Northern and Western Europe, with Norway at 45 percent (Newman et al., 2024: 17). The level of trust in news continues to be the highest in the Nordic region, as 55 percent of the surveyed in Norway "trust most news most of the time." The figure is 50 percent in Sweden, and as much as 69 percent and 57 percent in Finland and Denmark, respectively (Newman et al., 2024: 25). As for youth and news consumption in Norway, "there are some clouds on the horizon. It is hard to get young adults to subscribe" (Newman et al., 2024). These are key areas Schibsted Media is now focusing on. Siv Juvik Tveitnes, CEO of Schibsted Media, emphasizes the importance of maintaining on trust in combination with appealing to younger audiences (Juvik Tveitnes, interview with author, 2024).

Conclusion

In this last phase, 2017–2025, of Schibsted's digital transformation and international expansion, the dynamic between centralization and decentralization has had major consequences for the company. The external, company, and leadership dimensions give insight into this dynamic, and how the corporate strategies are shaped and how they are operationalized.

In terms of leadership dimensions, the style of management in this phase differed from the previous phase of strong centralization. The CEO of Schibsted, Kristin Skogen Lund, launched the Schibsted pyramid organization that positioned Schibsted as a company-wide foundation, providing support and investment for its subsidiaries. This represented a management style and strategy that aimed to be more aligned with the company's corporate culture characterized and shaped by autonomy and decentralization (Deslades, 2016: 313). This exemplifies how a shift in corporate strategy took place that aimed to combine and balance central corporate power and decision-making and autonomy and decentralized decision-making (Noam, 2019). Through the company-wide data

118 *Schibsted*

strategy, Schibsted aimed to achieve a competitive advantage against Google and Facebook. This exemplifies how, just as the global giants, large news media companies in the Nordic region benefit from size and scale (Lindberg, 2023). Schibsted was criticized in a similar way for its market power yet continued to expand its universe. As such, Schibsted became a regional platform giant, criticized, but also revered.

In terms of the external dimensions, the Nordic media system and market, it is clear that the company has benefited from the region's digital maturity and infrastructure and the rapid digital adoption rate within in its population. The media businesses have successfully extended their historical and traditional strong position to become primary digital news sources in the region, establishing themselves before the arrival of the global platforms, while in Asia, Latin America, and Africa, social media have become much more significant news destinations and even primary news sources (Lindberg, 2023). Similarly, already in the early 2000s, Schibsted and its newspapers succeeded in expanding their classified businesses and securing a dominant market position online in Norway, through the FINN company owned by the newspapers themselves. The success of the online classified advertising sites in the home market, was key to Schibsted's rapid international roll-out of this business. Combinared with the Swedish Blocket's disruptive business model and technology, Schibsted was able to exploit the fact that many international digital markets were far less mature than in the Nordic region.

In terms of the company dimension, the different opinions within the company leadership, combined with the market forces and the expectations of investors, contributed to pulling the company in different directions. While the Tinius Trust, the largest owner, with negative control over the company, had, through its Articles of Association, a specific focus on the news media, investors and the market were focused on the online classified advertising business. This exemplified a problematic side of trust or foundation ownership, in terms of limiting the possibilities for raising capital, growth, and expansion (Achtenhagen et al., 2018: 147). This eventually led to major changes in ownership form and company structure. The first solution was to spin out the international classified operation in Adevinta in 2019. Schibsted became the largest shareholder, as the new, major online classified company was listed, taking major financial positions in this classified advertising giant. This opened for far more flexible strategies for Adevinta and more strategic leeway for growth and capital raising, exemplified by the acquisition of eBay's Classified division, the largest acquisition in Norwegian financial history. Yet the Adevinta spin-off also played a role in the coming split of the Schibsted company.

The split in 2024 is the culmination of the strategic debate that has ridden the company for many years. The company finally gave up on achieving synergies between media and marketplaces in the Nordics, and on the idea of further centralization and integration of these two business areas. This reflects not only how the market forces pull in this direction but also the trend of foundations and trusts as leading acquirers of newspapers and thereby representing the key consolidating force. Instead, the rationale is to create synergies within Schibsted Media and within Schibsted Marketplaces. Schibsted also exemplifies the popularity yet ambiguous nature and unclear definition of the concept of ecosystem (Kostovska et al., 2020; Doyle, 2022), and how this has contributed to complicating the understanding of the corporate strategy and the operationalization of it. Schibsted has utilized two kinds of ecosystem strategies. The more geographically oriented ecosystems strategy emerged in the 2000s and was operationalized particularly in Sweden, but also Norway, while the global ecosystems strategy in the second half of the 2010s represented a data driven and product focused strategy. The running of two such ecosystem approaches contributed to making it complicated to understand and to operationalize Schibsted's corporate strategies.

7 Concluding Remarks – The Regional Perspective

In conclusion, we situate the digital transformation and international expansion of Schibsted within the global–local dichotomy – at the heart of the study of the internationalization and globalization of media and communication. This dichotomy entails an "uneasy" shifting "between a focus on the global scale of communication and upon the nation-state as its primary site of analysis and engagement" (Flew et al., 2016: 4). While some emphasize that the position of the nation in terms of media is diminishing in the face of the global (Castells, 2013; Chalaby, 2020), others argue for the nation's sustainability, persistence, and adaptability (Flew, 2020; Flew and Waisbord, 2015; Syvertsen et al., 2014; Mjos, 2022). A regional approach allows us to understand the development of Schibsted from two perspectives: from within the country-of-origin Norway and the Nordic region and from outside the region, and thereby also its international expansion.

Schibsted Seen From Within the Region

Taking the view of Schibsted from within the region, it becomes clear that the company is both seen as a cornerstone institution while at the same time is criticized by key stakeholders. Schibsted has a long tradition as a legacy newspaper company in Norway, and then Sweden, playing a central role in developing news and journalism and thereby also press freedom and freedom of speech in these societies. After being stock-listed in Norway, in 1992, the company expanded into TV and film, prior to the launch of a new vision and multimedia strategy in 1995. From the early forays into multimedia, and throughout the digital transformation and international expansion, Schibsted's size, controlling a large share of the Norway and Sweden's key newspapers and eventually a dominating position in online classified and marketplaces in these countries and internationally, as well as a major presence and recipient of profits from investments in classified operations internationally, made it a target for criticism in terms of its market and media power and threat to media diversity and pluralism. In fact, such criticism appeared already in the analog era, as the relationship between Norwegian authorities and the company became strained

DOI: 10.4324/9781003439431-7

Concluding Remarks – The Regional Perspective   121

in the 1990s. Schibsted's investments into local and regional newspapers raised fears for media pluralism and freedom of expression and culminated in the introduction of a law-limiting ownership to a maximum one-third of any specific market in Norway. Later, the formation of Norway's largest news media companies Media Norge (est. 2009) and later Schibsted Norge (est. 2012) was criticized by competitors for its media and market power, and threat to media diversity. In these cases, Schibsted has defended itself publicly, stating the need for consolidation and expansion to remain competitive and foster freedom of expression and media pluralism. Particularly in Norway, its main home market, Schibsted has had to balance carefully, aiming to avoid conflict with regulators: "Schibsted's executives publicly promote their views and argue that what is good for Schibsted is good for the Norwegian public and the principle of free speech (Syvertsen et al., 2014: 118).

Since the mid-2010s, as Facebook and Google's advertising market shares in the region increased dramatically, Schibsted has continued its public role and aimed to justify its strategies and actions, yet has continued to face criticism. Increasingly, the company has positioned itself as a defender of the values of the media system, by publicly criticizing the global platforms through op-ed pieces, debates, and hearings. Schibsted argues that media diversity, pluralism and freedom of speech, and the income to secure quality journalism are under threat, and furthermore, the global companies represent unfair competition, as they do not pay tax in the region. At the same time, Schibsted has turned itself into a Nordic giant. The company successfully launched its media and advertising platforms in the 2010s, a national, company-wide data strategy and data-driven ecosystem, the "Schibsted universe," into the 2020s, to secure a strong position and market share in both media and advertising in Norway and Sweden. Schibsted has argued publicly for increased collaboration between news media companies within Norway and the Nordic region, in the face of the expanding platform companies, while some competitors criticize Schibsted pointing to the company's size and market power.

By 2021, Schibsted's news division was one of the three dominating news companies in the region. These had grown in the past five to ten years through particularly mergers and acquisitions. These news media operations, owned by the Nordic media giants, Schibsted, Bonnier, and Sanomat, had over 50 percent of the total revenue of the top ten news companies. Schibsted has been a key player and driver of the considerable ownership concentration within the Nordic news sector (Lindberg, 2023), which has intensified throughout its digital transformation. By 2024, the issue of market and ownership concentration and media diversity is further actualized, when its largest owner, the Tinius Trust, acquired all Schibsted's media holdings in Norway and Sweden. The year after, Schibsted made major television and media acquisitions when purchasing TV4 in Sweden and MTV in Finland. This reflects two trends that work in combination within the region. First, foundations and trusts are now the leading acquirers of newspapers in the region and thereby a major consolidating

122 *Schibsted*

force (Sjovaag, 2019). By, 2025, six of the ten largest news media companies in the Nordic region are owned by foundations or trusts, and two of the top ten companies that are stock-listed had trusts as the largest single shareholder (Lindberg, 2023: 34–35). Second, the market forces are in many cases pulling toward specialization and not integration, in contrast to the strategy to achieve synergies across – and integration of – the media and online classfied advertising business areas, in the case of Schibsted.

The significance of the national and regional has been the key for media systems theory and how to understand media companies' expansion within a region, like the Nordic. Over ten years ago, Syvertsen et al. (2014) argued that the Nordic region's media system mirrored the characteristics of the strong welfare states of the region's countries. The four principles of the Nordic media system aim to counter the forces of globalization, authoritarianism, and marketization through the following four principles; the organization of key communication services in line with the concept of public goods with subsidies and requirements fostering universal access; the institutionalization of press freedom and self-governance of media; media policies that support media to ensure media diversity and quality; and last, collaboration and consensus between private and public actors, that is, the state, industries, and the public (Syvertsen et al., 2014: 120–121). By 2014, Schibsted's strategy, it was argued, resonated with all four principles. With reference to the last principle, Schibsted has been described as an "adaptive company," with an "adaptive strategy" in relation to the state, but also with the public. As a result, the company has achieved "high legitimacy in the public domain" which again has "justified by the firm's profile as a protector of free speech and a bulwark against foreign ownership" (Syvertsen et al., 2014: 105–106). Still, the split of Schibsted showed to some extent the limits of this adaptability as the core business areas: online classifieds and marketplaces and news media were separated, much in response to pressures from the market forces.

By 2025, as Schibsted's news media are close to being fully digital, it is clear that the company has benefited throughout its digital transformation from the region's digital infrastructure, created with the aim to provide universal access, and the rapid digital adoption rate among the region's population, to successfully extend their historically strong position in a region with the world's highest level of news consumption and to innovate to become a classified advertising winner. Already in the digital infancy, in the mid-1990s, Schibsted warned against international online companies becoming gatekeepers between its editorial content, advertising and readership. The traditional strong position of its news brands, coupled with rapid online expansion, contributed to them achieving similar positions within the digital domain, with direct relations with its readership and users. In fact, Schibsted's newspapers in Norway and Sweden, along with other news companies, have a position as primary digital news sources, in contrast to most international markets in which global platforms are now first destination for news consumption (Newman et al., 2024). In this way, the company is an important case also in terms of its role in the

Concluding Remarks – The Regional Perspective 123

region's societies with the world's highest level of press freedom and freedom of speech (RSF, 2024). However, these trends cannot be taken for granted. To succeed in becoming the leading Nordic media destination, the new Schibsted Media company sees it as imperative to retain trust between its news and media content and its users, and be able to attract a young audience. At the same time, the company must succeed in achiving profitability in a highly competitive market, shaped by platformization and unpredictable developments such as artificial intelligence. These are three of the main general challenges for news media in the digital era in this region and are of great significance for Schibsted's continuing position and role in these societies.

Schibsted Seen From Outside the Region

Looking at Schibsted's from the outside of the region, its digital transformation and international expansion, highlights three significant aspects.

First, the study of Schibsted provides a lens to understand the impact of competition in a region and how a company of such size and market position responds. While Schibsted has been criticized by competitors for its market power and potential threat to media diversity, Schibsted should also be considered as a bulwark, with a proactive strategy, in the face of the digital transformation and international competition. Already in the mid-1990s, Schibsted launched the regional Internet portal, *Scandinavia Online*, to be a first mover and take a dominant position in the home region, as similar portals emerged internationally. While the portal was sold, Schibsted's move into online classified in the late 1990s and early 2000s was the key to take a dominant classified advertising position in the home market with FINN in Norway, but also in Sweden, through Blocket, in the face of competition from national and international classified players. A key learning from the *Scandinavia Online* venture, was the legacy newspaper brands ability to achieve strong positions also in the digital market. As such, when global platforms arrived, Schibsted's online news brands and online classified advertising businesses had already been established for years in the region. Schibsted's launch of its Ecosystems strategy in the mid-2010s and the company-wide data strategy and its "Schibsted universe" in the late 2010s represented further regional competitive measures in the face of global platforms.

Second, its international expansion in classified advertising represents a lens in which to understand Schibsted's push outside its region. Interestingly, the four larges Nordic news companies each originate in one of the countries and have all expanded in various ways throughout the region and internationally: Schibsted (Norway), Bonnier (Sweden), Sanomat (Finland), and JP/Politikens Hus (Denmark) (Lindberg, 2023). Schibsted first created a solid position in the home market and its key international expansion began in Sweden. In 2003, having been unsuccessful in launching the Norwegian classified FINN in Sweden, Schibsted acquired, Blocket, the most successful

124   *Schibsted*

Swedish classified site. Blocket's technology and business model spearheaded the roll-out of Schibsted's classified operations internationally in markets that were not as developed as in the Nordics. In 2014, Schibsted had classified advertising sites in around 30 countries. The ambitious Ecosystem's strategy was launched in 2014, to compete with the global platforms. A key aim was to create a global online classified platform, yet its development failed, much due to lack of commitment from the different international classified sites, many operating autonomously in the different international markets. A further reason for the failure was related to the technology of the different sites. While it was the Blocket technology that had been originally rolled out in most places, as "Blocket clones," these sites had been further developed and adjusted over time and was not easily compatible with each other. This hampered the integration of national classified sites. In contrast to Facebook and Google, who distribute uniform, standardized products and technology worldwide, which was Schibsted's ideal, the company failed in successfully moving in this direction. This exemplifies the complexity of international expansion and the need to acknowledge the impact of national contexts and to balance central decision-making and strategy and the operationalization, with decentralized power and market realities.

Third, the internationalization of Schibsted also contributed to the downfall of the original structure of the company. While Schibsted has been labeled an "adaptive company" (Syvertsen et al., 2014), the split of the company in 2024, in some ways shows the limits of the company's ability to adapt its original structure of both media and classified advertising. The split of Schibsted, first through the spin-off of Adevitna, its internationally classified advertising operation, and then the following split between the Nordic marketplace business and the media business, was the culmination of a two decade-long discussion on the structure of the company. The Tinus Trust ownership, the largest owner with negative control of the company, long proved to safeguard the company from international takeover and secure long-term thinking throughout the digital transformation of the company. Yet as the company's internationalization intensified, it required capital raising, to acquire, develop, and market online classified advertising sites worldwide, while the company's media holdings were given far less financial priority. Such investments proved unpopular among investors and problematic for the Tinius Trust. The Tinius Trust had a defined focus on news media, but had to take part in the capital raising to retain its ownership share. The first solution to this issue was the spin-off of Adevinta, in 2019. The second solution, the splitting into Schibsted Media and Schibsted Marketplaces, in 2024, happened partly because the synergies between these two business areas were considered more difficult to achieve than synergies within each of the two business areas. As such, the international expansion, the lack of synergies within the region, along with the market forces, contributed to the splitting of the company. However, both the stock-listed Schibsted

Concluding Remarks – The Regional Perspective 125

marketplace and the Tinius Trust, owner of all media holdings, still have a presence outside the Nordic region, but only financially, through the Tinius Trust's around 22 per cent ownership of the issued shares, but nearly 30 per-cent of the voting rights, in Schibsted Marketplaces, that owns around 14 per-cent of the global online classified advertising company, Adevinta.

References

Achtenhagen, L., Melesko, S. and Ots, M. (2018) Upholding the 4th Estate . . . the Corporate Governance of the Media Ownership Form of Business Foundations. *International Journal on Media Management*, 20.

Adevinta (2018) *Schibsted Will Be Divided into Two Companies*. 18 September. https://adevinta.com/press-releases/schibsted-will-be-divided-into-two-companies/

Adevinta (2021) *Adevinta Completes Acquisition of eBay Classifieds Group*. 30 June. https://adevinta.com/press-releases/adevinta-completes-acquisition-of-ebay-classifieds-group/

Aldridge Lynum, O. (2014) *I år tjener Google 1,3 mrd. På våre nettsok*. 17 June. https://www.fvn.no/nyheter/okonomi/i/8V4e2/i-aar-tjener-google-13-mrd-paa-vaare-nettsoek

Anand, B. N. (2016) *The Content Trap: A Strategist's Guide to Digital Change*. New York: Random House.

Anand, B. N. and Hood, S. (2007) *Schibsted. Harvard Business School*. Case 707–474. April.

Artero, J. P. and Manfredi, J. L. (2016) Competences of Media Managers: Are they Special? Pp. 43–60. In G. F. Lowe and C. Brown (eds.), *Managing Media Firms and Industries, Media Business and Innovation*. Switzerland: Springer. https://doi.org/10.1007/978-3-319-08515-9_3

Barland, J. (2012) *Journalism for the Market. Product Development in VG and Aftonbladet on Print and Online 1995–2010*. Universitetet i Oslo.

Barland, J. (2013) Innovation of New Revenue Streams in Digital Media: Journalism as Customer Relationship. *Nordicom Review*, 34.

Barland, J. (2015) Innovation for New Revenue Streams from Digital Readers: The Case of *VG+*. *The Journal of Media Innovations*, 2(1). https://doi.org/10.5617/jmi.v2i1.952

Benson, R., Hessérus, M., Neff, T. and Sedel, J. (2025) *How Media Ownership Matters*. Oxford: Oxford University Press.

Bisgaard, A. (2014) *Ryssdal ruster opp mot Google*. 18 juli. https://kampanje.com/archive/medier/2014/07/presses-av-google-og-facebook/

Byttner, K. J. (2012) *Schibsted stuvar om hela portföljen*. https://www.resume.se/kommunikation/media/schibsted-stuvar-om-hela-portfoljen/?_x_tr_hist=true#social

Castells, M. (2013) *Communication Power*. New ed. Oxford: Oxford University Press.

References   127

Chalaby, J. K. (2020) Understanding Media Globalization: A Global Value Chain. Pp. 373–84. In S. Shimpach (ed.), *Analysis*. New York: Routledge, The Routledge Companion to Global Television.

Crampton, T. (2006) *European Search Engines Take on Google.* 17 December. https://www.nytimes.com/2006/12/17/technology/17iht-search.3927066.html

DESI (2022) *Digital Economy and Society Index.* European Commission. https://digital-strategy.ec.europa.eu/en/policies/desirsf

Deslades, G. (2016) Leadership in Media Organizations: Past Trends and Challenges Ahead. Pp. 311–327. In G. F. Lowe and C. Brown (eds.), *Managing Media Firms and Industries, Media Business and Innovation.* Switzerland: Springer. https://doi.org/10.1007/978-3-319-08515-9_10

DN (2001) *I McKinseys mektige nett.* 1 July. https://www.dn.no/i-mckinseys-mektige-nett/1-1-222343

DN (2007) *Felles front mot Schibsted.* 3 February. https://www.dn.no/etterbors/felles-front-mot-schibsted/1-1-883424

Doctor, K. (2013) *The Newsonomics of "Little Data," Data Scientists, and Conversion Specialists.* 17 October. https://www.niemanlab.org/2013/10/the-newsonomics-of-little-data-data-scientists-and-conversion-specialists/

Doyle, G. (2013) *Understanding Media Economics.* London, UK: SAGE.

Doyle, G. (2016) Managing in the Distinctive Economic Context of Media. Pp. 175–188. In G. F. Lowe and C. Brown (eds.), *Managing Media Firms and Industries, Media Business and Innovation.* Switzerland: Springer. https://doi.org/10.1007/978-3-319-08515-9_10

Doyle, G. (2022) Organisations as Ecosystems: The Case of Television Production. Pp. 80–92. In S. Baumann (ed.), *Handbook on Digital Business Ecosystems: Strategies, Platforms, Technologies, Governance and Societal Challenges.* Cheltenham: Edward Elgar Publishing.

eBay (2020) *Adevinta to Acquire eBay Classified Group to Create the World's Largest Online Classifieds Company.* 21 July. https://investors.ebayinc.com/investor-news/press-release-details/2020/Adevinta-to-Acquire-eBay-Classifieds-Group-to-Create-the-Worlds-Largest-Online-Classifieds-Company/default.aspx

Eckblad, B. (2018) *Schibsted svidde av milliarder i London. Nå har prestisjeprosjektet «Rocket» buklandet.* 30 September. https://www.dn.no/medier/teknologi/schibsted/rubrikk/schibsted-svidde-av-milliarder-i-london-na-har-prestisjeprosjektet-rocket-buklandet/2-1-426565

Eckblad, B. and Gjernes, K. (2017) *Inngikk verdensomspennende pakt med rubrikkrival.* 26 May. https://www.dn.no/magasinet/dokumentar/medier/schibsted/naspers/inngikk-verdensomspennende-pakt-med-rubrikk-rival/2-1-90380

Eckblad, B., Gjernes, K. and Tobiassen, M. (2017) *Sliter med gründersuksessene.* 5 mai. https://www.dn.no/teknologi/schibsted/schibsted-vekst/snapsale/sliter-med-grundersuksessene/2-1-77665

Eide, M. (1995) *Blod, sverte og gledestårer: VG, Verdens gang 1945–95.* Oslo: Schibsted Forlag.

Eide, M. (2008) Pressen – institusjoner og historie. Pp. 158–172. I M. Eide (ed.), *Medievitenskap: Medier – institusjoner og historie.* Bergen: Fagbokforlaget.

128 References

Eide, M. and Myrvang, C. (2018) *Alltid foran skjermen: Dagbladet og det digitale skiftet*. Oslo: Universitetsforlaget.

Eilertsen, F. (2015) *A Platform Future for Publishing, in Future Platforms for Independent Journalism*. Tinius Annual Report 2015.

Enli, G., Syvertsen, T. and Mjos, O. J. (2018) The Media Welfare State and the Media System: The Role of Media and Communications in the Evolution and Transformation of Scandinavian Welfare States. *Scandinavian Journal of History*, 43(5), 601–623. https://doi.org/10.1080/03468755.2018.1474023

Flew, T. (2020) Globalization, neo-globalization and post-globalization: The challenge of populism and the return of the national. *Global Media and Communication*, 16(1), 19–39.

Flew, T. and Waisbord, S. (2015) The Ongoing Significance of National Media Systems in the Context of Media Globalization. *Media, Culture & Society*, 37(4), 620–636. https://doi.org/10.1177/0163443714566903

Fossbakken, E. (2011) *VG+ er verdens beste Ipad-avis*. 11 October. https://kampanje.com/archive/2011/10/--vg-er-verdens-beste-ipad-avis/

Fossbakken, E. (2012) *Betalingsmur bremset opplagsfallet*. 16 November. https://kampanje.com/archive/2012/11/betalingsmur-bremset-opplagsfallet/

Fossen, E., Matre, J., Molstad, K., Rydne, N. and Zahl, J. (2024) *På tide å bla opp, Tinius*. 17 December. https://www.dn.no/innlegg/medier/arbeidsliv/schibsted/pa-tide-a-bla-opp-tinius/2-1-1754240

Godulla, A. and Böhm, S. (2023) Introduction. Pp. 1–16. In *Digital Disruption and Media Transformation. How Technological Innovation Shapes the Future of Communication*. Springer Nature Switzerland AG.

Golnaz Sadri, G. and Lees, B. (2001) Developing Corporate Culture as a Competitive Advantage. *Journal of Management Development*, 20(10), 853–859.

Gourevitch, S. and Deslandes, G. (2024) Digitalisation and the Need for a "Humanistic Turn" in Media Management. *Journal of Media Business Studies*, 1–20. https://doi.org/10.1080/16522354.2024.2307848

Hallin, D. C. and Mancini, P. (2004) *Comparing Media Systems: Three Models of Media and Politics*. Cambridge: Cambridge University Press.

Harland, J. H. (2018) *Securing Innovation through Corporate Spin-Off: An Exploratory Case Study. SNF Report No. 06/18*. Bergen, Norway. https://openaccess.nhh.no/nhh-xmlui/handle/11250/2597601

Hauger, K. K. (2012a) *Schibsted samler troppene i Norge*. 16 February. https://kampanje.com/archive/2012/02/schibsted-samler-troppene-i-norge/

Hauger, K. K. (2012b) *Starter med nettbetaling*. 23 May. https://kampanje.com/archive/2012/05/starter-med-nettbetaling/

Hauger, K. K. (2014) *Henter rubrikksjefer fra Schibsted*. 3 March. https://kampanje.com/archive/2014/03/henter-rubrikksjefer-fra-schibsted/

Hermanni, A. J. (2023) Business Models and Innovation Triggers in the Media Industry: How Digitalization Contributes to a Secure Future for Companies. Pp. 17–28. In A. Godulla and S. Böhm (eds.), *Digital Disruption and Media Transformation. How Technological Innovation Shapes the Future of Communication*. Springer Nature Switzerland AG.

Hjeltnes, G. (2010) Mot 2010: Imperiet vakler. Pp. 401–490. *I Norsk Presses Historie. Imperiet vakler*. Bind 3. Oslo: Universitetsforlaget.

Huseby Jensen, M. (2008) *Nettby ut i verden*. 3 April. https://www.nettavisen.no/nettby-ut-i-verden/s/12-95-1729313

References 129

Ibrus, I. (2024) 4 Media Innovation Studies: An Expanding Field. Pp. 43–58. In U. Rohn, M. Bjørn Rimscha and T. Raats (eds.), *De Gruyter Handbook of Media Economics*. Berlin, Boston: De Gruyter. https://doi.org/10.1515/9783110793444-004

Ihlebæk, K. A. and Sundet, V. S. (2021) Global Platforms and Asymmetrical Power: Industry Dynamics and Opportunities for Policy Change. *New Media & Society*. Online first. https://doi.org/10.1177/14614448211029662

Jerijervi, D. R. (2021) *Store endringer i Schibsted – Finn-sjefen får nye oppgaver.* 1 June. https://kampanje.com/medier/2021/06/finn-sjefen-slutter---far-nye-oppgaver-i-schibsted/

Kostovska, I., Raats, T., Donders, K. and Ballon, P. (2020) Going Beyond the Hype: Conceptualizing "Media Ecosystem" for Media Management Research. *Journal of Media Business Studies*, 18(1), 6–26. https://doi.org/10.1080/16522354.2020.1765668

Kraaijenbrink, J. (2020) *Strategy Consulting*. Cambridge: Cambridge University Press.

Krumsvik, A. H. (2006) What Is the Strategic Role of Online Newspapers? *Nordicom Review*, 27(2).

Krumsvik, A. H. (2014) Mulige modeller for fordeling av nettinntekter. *Norsk medietidsskrift*, 21(2).

Küng, L. (2016) Why is Media Management Research so Difficult – and What Can Scholars Do to Overcome the Field's Intrinsic Challenges? *Journal of Media Business Studies*, 13(4), 276–282. https://doi.org/10.1080/16522354.2016.1236572

Lindberg, T. (2023) *Nordic News Media in Global Competition: The Conditions for News Journalism in the Digital Platform Economy.* https://doi.org/10.48335/9789188855718

Lindblad (2021) *Annonsemarkedet etter Cookiedøden.* 12 Oktober. https://www.m24.no/cookies-debatt-facebook/annonsemarkedet-etter-cookiedoden/395928

Lowe, G. (2016) Introduction: What's So Special About Media Management? Pp. 1–20. In G. F. Lowe and C. Brown (eds.), *Managing Media Firms and Industries, Media Business and Innovation*. Switzerland: Springer. https://doi.org/10.1007/978-3-319-08515-9_1

McKenna, C. (2012) Strategy Followed Structure: Management Consulting and the Creation of a Market for "Strategy," 1950–2000. Pp. 153–186. In S. J. Kahl, B. S. Silverman and M. A. Cusumano (eds.), *History and Strategy, Advances in Strategic Management*, vol. 29. Leeds: Emerald Group Publishing Limited.

Medietilsynet (2023) *Norsk Medieøkonomi 2018–2022.* 28 June. https://www.medietilsynet.no/globalassets/publikasjoner/medieokonomi/231024_medieokonomi_2018-2022.pdf

Medietilsynet (2024) *Medieøkonomi: Økonomien i norske aviser 2019–2023.* 24 October. https://www.medietilsynet.no/globalassets/publikasjoner/medieokonomi/240627_avisenes_okonomi_2019-2023.pdf

Medina, M., Sánchez-Tabernero, A. and Arrese, Á. (2016) Contents as Products in Media Markets. In G. Lowe and C. Brown (eds.), *Managing Media Firms and Industries. Media Business and Innovation*. Cham: Springer. https://doi.org/10.1007/978-3-319-08515-9_14

130 References

Mjos, O. J. (2010) *Media Globalization and the Discovery Channel Networks.* London, New York: Routledge.

Mjos, O. J. (2012) *Music, Social Media and Global Mobility: MySpace, Facebook and YouTube.* London, New York: Routledge.

Mjos, O. J. (2022) *An Introduction to Global Media for the Twenty-First Century.* London: Bloomsbury Academic.

Mossin, B. Å. (2015) *Schibsted dro inn 2,6 milliareder på få timer.* 10 September. https://www.journalisten.no/trond-berger-schibsted-media-group-schibsted/schibsted-dro-inn-26-milliarder-pa-fa-timer/307977

Newman, N., Fletcher, R., Robertson, C. T., Ross Arguedas, A. and Kleis Nielsen, R. (2024) *Reuters Digital News Report 2024.* Reuters Institute for the Study of Journalism. https://reutersinstitute.politics.ox.ac.uk/sites/default/files/2024-06/RISJ_DNR_2024_Digital_v10%20lr.pdf

Nielsen, R. K. and Fletcher, R. (2023) Comparing the Platformization of News Media Systems: A Cross-Country Analysis. *European Journal of Communication*, 38(5), 484–499. https://doi.org/10.1177/02673231231189043

Nielsen, R. K. and Ganter, S. A. (2022) *The Power of Platforms: Shaping Media and Society.* Oxford: Oxford University Press.

Noam, E. M. (2019) *Managing Media and Digital Organizations.* Cham: Palgrave Macmillan. https://doi.org/10.1007/978-3-319-71288-8_14

Norland, A. (2001) *Bly blir gull: Schibsteds historie 1839–1933.* Bind 1. Oslo: Schibsted.

Norland, A. (2011) *Medier, makt og millioner: Schibsteds historie 1934–2011.* Bind 2. Oslo: Schibsted.

O'Brian, D. (2024) 30 the Transformation of News in the Digital Age: Business Model Changes, Challenges, and Future Directions. Pp. 431–450. In U. Rohn, M. B. Rimscha and T. Raats (eds.), *De Gruyter Handbook of Media Economics.* Berlin, Boston: De Gruyter. https://doi.org/10.1515/9783110793444-017

Oliver, J. J. and Picard, R. G. (2020) Shaping the Corporate Perimeter in a Changing Media Industry. *International Journal on Media Management*, 22(2), 67–82. https://doi.org/10.1080/14241277.2020.1716767

O'Reilly III, C. A. and Tushman, M. L. (2008) Ambidexterity as a dynamic capability: Resolving the innovator's dilemma. *Research in Organizational Behavior*, 28, 185–206.

Ottosen, R. and Krumsvik, A. H. (2012) Digital Challenges on the Norwegian Media Scene. *Nordicom Review*, 33(2), 43–55.

Picard, R. G. (2010) The Future of the News Industry. Pp. 365–379. In J. Curran (eds.), *Media and Society.* London: Bloomsbury Academic.

Poell, T., Nieborg, D. and van Dijck, J. (2019) Platformisation. *Internet Policy Review*, 8, 4. https://doi.org/10.14763/2019.4.1425

Poell T, Nieborg D. B. and Duffy B. E. (2021) *Platforms and Cultural Production.* Cambridge: Polity.

RSF (2024) *World Press Freedom Index. Reporters Without Borders.* https://rsf.org/en/2024-world-press-freedom-index-journalism-under-political-pressure

Ryssdal, R. E. (2016) *Samarbeid er nødvendig i kampen om annonsekronene.* Rolv Erik Ryssdal, CEO Schibsted Media Group. 30 juni. *Aftenposten*, p. 13.

Schibsted (1995–2005) *Annual Report.* https://reports.huginonline.com/hugin/

References 131

Schibsted (2006a) *Schibsted Annual Report*. http://hugin.info/131/R/1121345/206446.pdf

Schibsted (2006b) *Decision to establish Media Norge*. 22 December. https://schibsted.com/releases/schibsted-asa-sch-decision-to-establish-media-norge/

Schibsted (2006c) *Media Norge to be established without Adresseavisen ASA*. 15 December. https://schibsted.com/releases/schibsted-asa-sch-media-norge-to-be-established-without-adresseavisen-asa/

Schibsted (2007) *Schibsted Annual Report 2007*. http://hugin.info/131/R/1208961/249675.pdf

Schibsted (2008) *Annual Report*. https://www.annualreports.co.uk/HostedData/AnnualReportArchive/s/schibsted-asa_2008.pdf

Schibsted (2009a) *Divestment of Metronome Film & Television AB*. 28 April. https://schibsted.com/releases/schibsted-asa-sch-divestment-of-metronome-film-television-ab-detailed-stock-exchange-announcement/

Schibsted (2009b) *Annual Report 2009*. https://www.annualreports.com/HostedData/AnnualReportArchive/s/schibsted-asa_2009.pdf

Schibsted (2010) *Schibsted Classified Media. Capital Markets Day*. https://static.schibsted.com/wp-content/uploads/Global/Financial%20documents/CMD/CMD%202010/CMD%202010%208%20SCM%20final.pdf

Schibsted (2012) *Annual Report*. https://static.schibsted.com/wp-content/uploads/Global/SCH_Annual_2012_EN_text.pdf

Schibsted (2013) *Sverre Munck Steps Down, Frode Eilertsen New EVP Strategy and Digital Transformation*. https://schibsted.com/news/sverre-munck-steps-down-frode-eilertsen-new-evp-strategy-and-digital-transformation/

Schibsted (2014a) *Annual Report*. http://hugin.info/131/R/1911430/682298.pdf

Schibsted (2014b) *Strengthening Focus on Growth*. 1 February. https://schibsted.com/news/strenghtening-focus-on-growth/

Schibsted (2014c) *Google Tech Executive Joins Schibsted*. 8 May. https://schibsted.com/news/google-tech-executive-joins-schibsted/

Schibsted (2014d) *Adam Kinney, Former Google and Twitter, is Appointed Head of Data Science at Schibsted*. 12 November. https://schibsted.com/news/adam-kinney-new-head-of-data-science-in-schibsted-media-group/

Schibsted (2015a) *What to Join Schibsted's Tech Adventure in London?* 10 March. https://schibsted.com/news/want-to-join-schibsteds-new-tech-adventure-in-london/

Schibsted (2015b) *SvD Successfully Launching on Schibsted Media Platform*. 27 May. https://schibsted.com/news/svd-successfully-launching-on-schibsted-media-platform/

Schibsted (2015c) *Schibsted Annual Report*. https://www.annualreports.com/HostedData/AnnualReportArchive/s/schibsted-asa_2015.pdf

Schibsted (2016) *Driving Long Term Online Growth*. Schibsted Media Group Investor Day, London and New York. 27–28 September. https://schibsted.com/releases/schibsted-asa-scha-schb-investor-day-2016-driving-long-term-online-growth/

Schibsted (2017) *How Schibsted Builds Its Own Publishing Platform*. 10 February. https://www.schibsted.pl/news/schibsted-publishing-platform/

Schibsted (2018a) *One Becomes Two: A Leading Digital Growth Company and a Global Leader in Online Classifieds*. 18 September. http://hugin.info/131/R/2216648/865847.pdf

132 References

Schibsted (2018b) *Schibsted CEO Reveals New Management Team.* 19 December. https://schibsted.com/releases/schibsted-ceo-reveals-new-management-team/

Schibsted (2020) *Schibsted Acquires Sanoma's Online Classifieds' Business Oikotie in Finland.* 16 July. https://schibsted.com/news/schibsted-acquires-sanomas-online-classifieds-business-oikotie-in-finland/

Schibsted (2021a) *PodMe to become Schibsted's Premium Podcast Hub.* 8 June. https://schibsted.com/news/podme-to-become-schibsteds-premium-podcast-hub/

Schibsted (2021b) *Schibsted's Line Classified in Denmark Moves Forward.* 25 June. https://schibsted.com/releases/schibsted-schibsted-asa-scha-schb-schibsteds-online-classified-investment-in-denmark-moves-forward/

Schibsted (2022a) *Ole Jacob Sunde, Chair of Schibsted 2002–2022.* Oslo: Schibsted.

Schibsted (2022b) *Annual Report 2021.* https://static.schibsted.com/wp-content/uploads/2022/04/07164038/Schibsted-Annual-Report-2021.pdf

Schibsted (2022c) *Schibsted samler sine norske nyhetsmedier i ny "superbundle."* 20 October. https://schibsted.com/news/schibsted-samler-sine-norske-nyhetsmedier-i-ny-superbundle/

Schibsted (2023a) *Annual Report 2023.* https://cdn.schibsted.com/wp-content/uploads/2024/05/13130115/Schibsted-Annual-Report-2023.pdf

Schibsted (2023b) *A Perfect Match. Future Report 2024.* November. https://futurereport.schibsted.com/a-perfect-match/

Schibsted (2023c) *Schibsted Supports the Voluntary Offer for Adevinta Reducing Its Stake in Adevinta by 60 %.* 21 November. https://schibsted.com/news/schibsted-supports-the-voluntary-offer-for-adevinta-reducing-its-stake-in-adevinta-by-60/

Schibsted (2023d) *Schibsted Initiates Process to Sell Its News Media Operations to the Tinius Trust.* 11 December. https://schibsted.com/news/schibsted-initiates-process-to-sell-its-news-media-operations-to-the-tinius-trust/

Schibsted (2024a) *Schibsted and Tinius Trust Sign Final Agreement on Sale of Its News Operations.* 22 March. https://schibsted.com/news/schibsted-and-tinius-trust-sign-final-agreement-on-sale-of-news-media-operations/

Schibsted (2024b) *Schibsted Buys Polaris 9.99 Stake in Finn.* 26 April. https://schibsted.com/news/schibsted-buys-polaris-9-99-stake-in-finn/

Schibsted (2024c) *Schibsted ASA Announces Management Changes.* 28 May. https://schibsted.com/news/schibsted-asa-announces-management-changes/

Schibsted (2024d) *The Road Ahead for Schibsted Marketplaces.* 31 May. https://schibsted.com/2024/05/31/the-road-ahead-for-schibsted-marketplaces/

Schibsted (2024e) *Schibsted Marketplaces Advances Its Simplification Efforts.* 23 October. https://schibsted.com/news/schibsted-marketplaces-advances-its-simplification-efforts/

Schibsted Media (2024) *Schibsted Media-sjefen: «En ny epoke».* 10 October. https://e24.no/naeringsliv/i/LMdmRJ/schibsted-media-kutter-rundt-350-aarsverk

Schibsted Media (2025a) *The AI-Futures We Bet On.* 27 January. https://schibstedmedia.com/news/the-ai-futures-we-bet-on/

Schibsted Media (2025b) *Schibsted Media Agrees to Acquire TV4 in Sweden and MTV in Finland From Telia Company.* 25 February. https://

References 133

schibstedmedia.com/news/schibsted-media-agrees-to-acquire-tv4-in-sweden-and-mtv-in-finland-from-telia-company/

Scholtz Nærø, S. (2005) *Tinius. Om medier, milliarder og hunden Tott*. Oslo: Kagge Forlag.

Sesam (2005) *Search Seminar*. 22 November. http://hugin.info/131/R/1022360/161665.pdf

Sjøvaag, H. (2014) Homogenisation or Differentiation? The Effects of Consolidation in the Regional Newspaper Market. *Journalism Studies*, 15(5), 511–521. https://doi.org/10.1080/1461670X.2014.885275

Sjøvaag, H. (2015) Introducing the Paywall: A Case Study of Content Changes in Three Online Newspapers. *Journalism Practice*, 10(3), 304–322. https://doi.org/10.1080/17512786.2015.1017595

Sjøvaag, H. (2019) *Journalism between the State and the Market*. London, New York: Routledge.

Sjøvaag, H. (2023) *The Markets for News: Enduring Structures in the Age of Business Model Disruptions*. London, New York: Routledge.

Sjøvaag, H. and Ohlsson, J. (2019) Media Ownership and Journalism. *Oxford Research Encyclopedia of Communication*. Retrieved 18 April 2023, from https://oxfordre.com/communication/view/10.1093/acrefore/9780190228613.001.0001/acrefore-9780190228613-e-839

Solgård, J. (2025) Schibsted Media-sjefen forsvarer oppkjøp midt i store kostnadskutt: – Vi kan ikke finansiere driften med sparepenger. 25 February. https://www.dn.no/marked/schibsted-media/medier/schibsted-media-sjefen-forsvarer-oppkjop-midt-i-store-kostnadskutt-vi-kan-ikke-finansiere-driften-med-sparepenger/2-1-1784073

Spigseth, R. (2008) *Frykter følgende av Media Norge*. 27 February. https://www.dagsavisen.no/kultur/2008/02/27/frykter-folgene-av-media-norge/

Storsul, T. and Krumsvik, A. H. (2013) What is Media Innovation? Pp. 13–26. In T. Storsul and A. H. Krumsvik (eds.), *Media Innovations: A Multidisciplinary Study of Change*. Göteborg: Nordicom.

Sundin, S. (2013) *Den svenske mediamarknaden*. Göteborg: Nordicom.

Syvertsen, T. (2004) *Mediemangfold: Styring av mediene i et globalisert marked*. Kristiansand: IJ-Forlaget.

Syvertsen, T., Moe, H., Mjøs, O. J. and Enli, G. (2014) *The Media Welfare State: Nordic Media in the Digital Era*. Ann Arbour: University of Michigan Press.

Tobiassen, M. and Øvrebo Johanessen, S. (2014) *Angriper Googles skattefordel*. 6 July. https://www.dn.no/skatt/oecd/skatterett/facebook/angriper-googles-skattefordel/1-1-5145096

Waatland, E. (2024) *Nordens mediegiganter samler seg – Men hvor er Schibsted?* 4 December. https://www.m24.no/amedia-bonnier-erik-waatland/nordens-mediegiganter-samler-seg-men-hvor-er-schibsted/775866

WAN-IFRA (2017) *How Schibsted Media Group Makes Disruption Seem Hip*. 18 May. https://wan-ifra.org/2017/05/how-schibsted-media-group-makes-disruption-seem-hip/

Wekre, H. (2007) *Ikke redd for Facebook*. 4 May. https://www.nettavisen.no/ikke-redd-for-facebook/s/12-95-1009879

Westlund, O., Krumsvik, A. H. and Lewis, S. C. (2020) Competition, Change, and Coordination and Collaboration: Tracing News Executives' Perceptions About Participation in Media Innovation. *Journalism Studies*, 22(1), 1–21. https://doi.org/10.1080/1461670X.2020.1835526

Index

+Alt 104–105
20 Minutes 30, 48, 51, 55

Aamot, Kjell 17–18, 20–21, 22, 23, 24, 32–36, 41, 42, 46, 47, 55, 56, 58, 61, 62, 63, 79
Adevinta 1, 2, 100, 101, 106–109, 111, 112, 118, 124, 125
Adresseavisen 30–31, 39, 52, 54
advertising: and online news 29–31; and search 50–51; classified 30–31, 38, 39–44, 48–50; display 70, 106; identity-based 82; national markets and 18, 30–31; online news and 102; print newspapers and 8, 55; social media and 85, 91, 116; user data and 84, 102, 105
advertising technology 105–106
Aftenposten 15–18, 31, 35, 39, 40, 41, 44, 45, 52, 53, 64, 65, 67–68, 79, 85, 90, 101, 109, 111, 114; digital subscriptions and 72, 104, 105
Aftonbladet 16, 27–30, 35, *39*, 44, 46; Blocket.se and 73; growth and 77–78
Agerup, Karl Christian 108
Alma Media 47, 50
Amandus project 24
Amandus trainee program 32–35, 47–48, 59
Amedia 10, 104–105
America Online 24, 45
artificial intelligence (AI) 115, 123
authoritarianism *see* Media Welfare State

autonomous strategies 6
Avis1 30

Bain & Company 9–10
Bergens Tidende 30, 31, 39, 52–53, 65, 67, 104
Blackstone 108–109
Blocket 46, 55, 73, 86, 93, 99, 123–124; Blocket clones 48, 55, 64, 124; business model and 59; international expansion and 48–49; technology and 44, 48
Blommenholm Industrier 2, 26, 106
Bonnier 10, 47, 78, 116
Boston Consulting Group 9–10
Brazil 75–77, 98, 106

centralized strategies 6, 9
Chile 76
classified advertising online 30–31; Adevinta and 106–107; ecosystem and platform strategy and 86–87
content marketing 105–106
corporate culture 9
corporate strategy 5–6, *7*; capital and financial conditions and 12; company dimensions and 10–11; corporate culture and 9; external dimensions and 6–8; global management consultancies and 9–10; innovation and 12–13; leadership dimensions and 8–9; organizational structure and 11–12
creative destruction 13, 59

Index 135

Dagbladet 70, 91
data ecosystems 83, 113; *see also* ecosystem
decentralized strategies 6, 9
Denmark 16, 102, 108, 117
diagonal expansion 11
digital business models: cost-cutting and 61–65; growth and 77–79; news media and 65–73; online classifieds and marketplaces and 73–77; ecosystems and platforms and 82, 87, 94, 96; digital subscriptions and content marketing and 103–106
digital expansion: dot-com crash and 38–39; FINN and 39–43; international vision and 46–48; news media and 44–46; summary of 58–60; Swedish 43–44
digitization: internationally 38; Nordic region and 44, 52; Norway and 22, 70, 80; Sweden and 20–21
dot.com crisis, the 38–39, 45, 62

eBay 102, 107
ecosystem: as strategy 82–83, 119; challenges of 92–94; data-driven 123; global 97; international classified advertising and 86–87; media and classifieds 87–92; news media and 83–86; summary of 94–96
Eilertsen, Frode 83, 94
Eilertsen, T. 65–67, 72
Estonia 22
Expressen 28

Facebook 63, 79, 82, 90; advertising and 83–86, 95, 121 (*see also* social media); competition and 1, 4; expansion and 59, 63; platform-dependency and 91
Facebook Marketplaces 86
Fædrelandsvennen 30, 39, 52, 71–72, 81
financial crisis, the 55–61, 64
Finland 2, 3, 47, 102, 104, 108, 110, 113, 116–117, 123

FINN 31, 38–42, 92, 98–103, 110, 113, 123; innovation and 41–43, 68; network effect and 43–44, 59–60
Finnmer 43, 44
foundation ownership 10–11
France 30, 48–49, 55, 74, 112, 117
free newspapers internationally 14, 24, 29–30, 39, 46, 48, 49, 55
freedom of speech 3, 7, 95, 116, 120–123
Frydenlund, Kåre 24
full access subscription 104–105

Germany 30, 34, 49, 117
global management consultancies 9–10
global-local dichotomy 2, 4–5, 120
globalization 7, 89, 120, 122; *see also* Media Welfare State
Google 59, 63, 79, 90, 121; advertising and 82, 83–85, 95; competition and 60; news products and 51; platform-dependency and 91
Google News 51, 85–86
Gota Media 10
Gravir, Sondre 53, 67, 85–87, 92, 93, 98
Grünthal, Raoul 63, 78, 79, 98, 100, 111, 112, 115

Hallingdølen 71
Harstad Tidende Group 54
Hjertnes, Øyulf 67
Holter-Hovind, Bjørn A. 26, 33
horizontal expansion 11

initial public offering (IPO) 19, 111, 118
innovation 12–13
international expansion 123; classified advertising and 48–50; European media 50–55; financial crises and 55–58; new vision and 46–48; summary of 58–60
internationalization strategy 21–24; *Aftonbladet* and *Svenska*

136 *Index*

Dagbladet 27–29; classified advertising online and 30–31; online editions 29; *Scandinavia Online* (SOL) 24–26; Tinius Trust and 26–27
internet portals 24, 36; *see also* Scandinavia Online (SOL)

journalism 12, 60, 114, 120–121, JP/Politikens HUS 10
Juvik Tveitnes, Siv 67, 88, 90, 98, 100, 114, 116, 117
Jysk Fynske Medier 10

Koch, Per Axel 52, 110
Kvasir 25, 50

Langbraaten, Anne 20
leadership dimensions 8–9, 58
Leboncoin 49, 73–74, 86
Lendo Group 78, 110, 113
Liebenberg, Rian 83, 88, 89, 94
Local News Consortium, The 102
London 87, 94, 112
Loken Stavrum, Kristin 19, 27

Magnus, Birger 17, 22–23, 25–26, 28, 33, 36, 42, 46–48, 56–58, 62, 67, 79
Matre, Hans Erik 67
management style 8–9, 23, 34, 35, 36, 52, 58, 95, 110
market competition 7–8
marketization *see* Media Welfare State
Markussen, J. A. 54–55
McKinsey & Company 9–10, 23, 36–37, 60, 70, 83, 108, 110
media innovation 13
Media Norge 53, 52–58, 65, 66–67, 70, 80, 89, 91, 121
media policy 19; *see also* Media Welfare State, The
media system *see* Media Welfare State
Media Welfare State, The 3, 6–7, 122
Metro 30
MTV 116, 121

Munch, Didrik 31, 40, 52, 57, 67, 69–71, 72, 83, 99, 100
Munck, Sverre 22, 25, 30–31, 33, 36, 41, 42, 45, 46, 48, 49, 52, 74, 75, 76, 83, 92
Murdoch, Rupert 55–56

Nagell-Erichsen, Tinius 18, 19, 20–21, 26–27, 34, 35, 36, 46, 62; *see also* Tinius Trust
Naspers 74–77
Nettby 51, 59, 84, 86
network effects 5, 8, 33, 41–44, 59
New York Times 104
news media 44–46; ecosystem and platform strategy and 83–86; platforms and 86, 91, 117
newspapers 3, 8, 10, 12, 14, 39; in society 7, 15–16
Nordic marketplaces 102–103, 108–113
Nordic media houses 103–104, 108–113
Nordic media market: first phase 3; fourth phase 4; second phase 3; third phase 3–4
Nordic region: media system of 121–122; news companies and 83; trust in the news 117; view of Schibsted from 120–121
Norrköpings Tidningars Media 10
Norway; society and 14–15, 35; media market and 3, 4, 15, 16, 29, 48, 114–117; online classified advertising and 39–43, 113–114; politics and 2, 3, 15, 16, 116–117

OLX 75
One Company strategy 87–88, 95–96; *see also* ecosystem and platform strategy
online classified advertising 38, 118; FINN and 39–44; international expansion of 48–50; ecosystem and platform and 82, 83, 86–89, 92–94; Schibsted Marketplaces and 102–103, 113–114; Adevinta and 106–109

Index 137

online newspaper editions 4, 29–30
online subscription 70–71, 103–105
organizational ambidexterity *see*
structural ambidexterity
organizational structure 11–12
Orkla 19, 20
OsloNett 25, 50
ownership strcuture and form 10–11,
14, 16–20, 36, 76, 97, 118

paywalls 4, 71–72, 91
Pedersen, Torry 25, 26, 29, 45, 69
Permira 108–109
platformization 4, 82, 122;
dependency and 91; dominance
and 4, 93; expansion and 4, 123
podcasts 104, 109
Polaris Media 54, 109–110, 116
political parties 15–16
press: editorial freedom and 15;
ownership and 10–11, 14, 16–20;
party press and 15–16; press
freedom and 3, 116, 120, 122
press subsidies 7, 15–16
Principal-Agent Problem 9, 59, 80
Printzell Halvorsen, Christian 87, 90,
91, 93, 103, 110, 111
private equity 108–109
professional ownership 19
public service broadcasting 104

resource allocation 12
Rocket project 92–93
Rosinski, Aleksander 23, 24, 41, 49,
74, 75, 76, 107
Russia 55
Ryssdal, Rolv Erik 18, 19, 27, 28, 48,
49, 62–64, 66, 85, 94, 107, 115

Samuelson, Lena 46
Sanoma 10, 102, 121, 123
Scandinavia Online (SOL) 24–26,
36, 45; *see also* Internet portals
Schibsted Classified Media (SCM)
64, 73–74
Schibsted Growth 77–79
Schibsted Marketplaces 2, 87, 98,
113–114, 124

Schibsted Marketplaces International
(MPI) 98–100
Schibsted Media 2, 98, 100, 109,
113, 114–117, 122–123
Schibsted Media Platform (SMP)
89, 90
Schibsted Next 100, 102–103, 111
Schibsted Norge 65, 66, 67, 69–70,
71, 80, 91–92, 121
Schibsted organization: Adevinta
and 106–107; content marketing
and advertising technology
105–106; Nordic media houses
and 103–104; post-ecosystem
strategies 97–101; pyramid and
101–102; subscriptions and user
payment 104–105; verticalization
and 102–103; *see also* Schibsted
Sverige, Schibsted Norge,
Schibsted Growth, Media Norge,
Schibsted Media and Schibsted
Marketplaces.
Schibsted Products and Technology
83, 88, 89, 100
Schibsted pyramid 101–102
Schibsted split 108–109; deals
shaping the 109–110; reasons for
110–113
Schibsted Sverige/Sweden 58, 63,
69, 77, 78–80, 83, 91, 99, 115
Schibsted universe 102, 103, 105,
106, 121
Schibsted, Christian 1, 15
search engines 25, 50–51, 58–60,
116; *see also* Sesam
Seljeseth, Terje 31, 39, 40, 88, 89
Sesam 1, 51, 56, 58, 60, 85–86; *see
also* search engines
share split 87–88
Sigma project 108, 112–113
Singapore 77
Skogen Lund, Kristin 65, 67, 68,
101–106, 111, 112, 115
social media 91, 116–117; *see also*
Facebook; Nettby
Spain 30, 48, 51, 55
Stavanger Aftenblad 30
Steen, Birger 24

138 *Index*

Steiro, Gard 67, 68, 70, 71, 72, 78, 79, 85, 88, 115
Stromblad, Gunnar 27, 46
structural ambidexterity 69
structural autonomy 67–69
Sunde, Ole Jacob 20, 26–27, 33, 34, 35, 36, 41, 42, 46, 50, 57, 58, 62, 63, 77, 84, 93, 98, 99, 108, 111, 114
Sunstone project 103, 110, 113
Svenska Dagbladet 27–30, 35, 46, 77–78
Sweden: media market and 16, 28–29, 48, 77–79, 114–117; online classified advertising and 43–44, 113–114; politics and 2, 3, 15, 16, 116–117

Telenor 25, 76–77
television 3, 41–42, 63, 116
TikTok 116
Tilväxtmedier 77–79, 114
Tinius Trust 1–2, 63, 108–109, 114, 121, 124; Articles of Association and 2, 111–112, 118; internationalization strategy and 26–27; ownership structure and 76, 87–88, 97; *see also* Nagell-Erichsen, Tinius
Thorsheim, Andreas 67

Trader Classified Media 49–50, 56, 74
Trafikfonden 78, 81
trust 3, 117, 123
trust ownership 9–10
TV2 18, 19, 33, 46, 47, 50, 63, 116
TV4 50, 63, 116
TVNorge 22

United States 15, 16, 24, 30, 102, 117
user payment 104–105; *see also* paywall

Verdens Gang (VG) 15–18, 29, 35, 39, 44, 78, 79, 84, 85, 101, 106, 109; *VG Nett* 39, 43, 46, 69; *VG+* and 72; *VGTV* 69–70, 81, 89; *VG Mobil* 69, 81
vertical expansion 11
verticalization 102–103, 110–111, 113; *see also* Schibsted Marketplaces
Viktklubben 71

World War II 15

X (Twitter) 83, 95, 116

Yahoo! 45, 51

Printed in the United States
by Baker & Taylor Publisher Services